THOUGHTS ARE YOUR *Reality*

WILLIE SEALS

Copyright © 2024 Willie Seals.

All rights reserved. No part of this book may be reproduced, stored, or transmitted by any means—whether auditory, graphic, mechanical, or electronic—without written permission of both publisher and author, except in the case of brief excerpts used in critical articles and reviews. Unauthorized reproduction of any part of this work is illegal and is punishable by law.

ISBN: 979-8-89419-164-5 (sc)
ISBN: 979-8-89419-165-2 (hc)
ISBN: 979-8-89419-166-9 (e)

Because of the dynamic nature of the Internet, any web addresses or links contained in this book may have changed since publication and may no longer be valid. The views expressed in this work are solely those of the author and do not necessarily reflect the views of the publisher, and the publisher hereby disclaims any responsibility for them.

One Galleria Blvd., Suite 1900, Metairie, LA 70001
(504) 702-6708

CONTENTS

Achieve 1
Action 2
Adequate 3
Advice 4
Afraid 5
Annoying 6
Anger 7
Appreciate 8
Awaken 9
Behind 10
Being Mad 11
Belief 12
Calling 13
Chance 14
Challenge Yourself 15
Change 16
Choose Happiness 17
Circumstance 18
Clarity 19
Coach 20
Comfort 21
Compete 22
Confidence 23
Conflict 24
Create Your Life 25
Deception 26
Decision 27
Destiny 28
Difficulties 29
Educate 30
Ego 31
Enemy 32
Experience 33

Expert 34
Flexibility 35
Free 36
Free To Be You 37
Frequency! 38
Fulfillment 39
Future 40
Giving and Receiving 41
Goals 42
Help 43
Helping! 44
Ignorance 45
Imagine 46
Impact 47
Instincts 48
It's In You! 49
Karma 50
Keep Encouraged my Sistahs! 51
Kindness 52
Basic Knowledge 53
Knowledge 54
Limitations 55
Live, Love, Laugh 56
Magnet 57
Mentorship 58
Move ON 59
Multiplier 60
Navigation 61
Negative Thinking 62
Obstacle 63
Openness 64
Opportunities 65
Optimism 66
Pay Attention 67
Persuasion 68
Plan 69
Possible 70

Promises	71
Purpose	72
Rejuvenate	73
Responsibility	74
Sanity or Insanity	75
Show	76
The State of the World	77
Stay Positive	78
Stop Hating	79
Structure	80
Struggling	81
Supporting	82
Teachers	83
Team	84
Teamwork	85
The Law	86
The Power of Love	87
Think	88
Thoughts!	89
Titles	90
Tomorrow	91
Transition	92
Trouble	93
Trust Yourself	94
Understand	95
Upsetting	96
Vision	97
Wait	98
Where is your Pride?	99
Why (1)	100
Wisdom	101
Work Ethic	102
World Gone Mad	103
Worry	104
Youth	105

Mind
ACHIEVE

The only way to achieve anything is to believe in yourself first. You can achieve whatever you desire in life. God has given us the wisdom for our beliefs to manifest. We just sell ourselves short sometimes by giving up. We must learn when things become hard in life to stay focused. People will tell you that you cannot do this, but don't listen to them. Whatever you do in life you must be able to see yourself doing for a lifetime. When you are doing what you love, you will attract more things of value. Then, help share with others who need them. You will always achieve more when you're a happy giver. Change your thoughts in feelings. They have the power to either raise or lower your vibration, and the higher your vibe, the better your life. Keep loving what you do in life, and you will surely reach greater heights than you can ever imagine. Focus on every positive thought, and you will see those thoughts become your reality. Block the world out, and let God guide you. There isn't a problem you cannot cope with. God has giving you the capability to create whatever environment you choose. Tell yourself, "I am a creator, and I am powerful! My life deserves nothing but greatness!" Determination, commitment, and self-discipline enable you to overcome any obstacle, reach any goal, and fulfill your purpose in life. The energy of the mind is the essence of life!

Head Shepherd
P.O.G.
Loving Ministry

Mind
ACTION

To make a difference in your life, you must take action. Just speaking about what you want to do isn't enough. Faith without action is dead. That's what the Good Book says. If you look back over your life, you will see every time there was a change, you took action in order to make it happen. Stop dreaming about it and *be* about it! If at some point if you don't build your dream someone else will hire you to help build theirs. There is no failure, it is just a lesson and training for your mind. The stronger your mindset is, the greater your skill set is going to be. Always be a positive person. This is your life that you are fighting for. Don't wait for someone to make it happen. *You* must make it happen. Knowing is not enough. We must apply. Willing is not enough. We must do. What makes dreams into reality? I believe that perhaps the most important, and often most ignored, thing is simply taking action. If you want to achieve your goals, you need to shift from dreaming to doing. Taking action means laying out a plan to achieve your goals and putting in a consistent effort to achieve them. Over time, you can make the vision of your dreams real. When your goals are too vague, you'll have a difficult time making them happen. Getting a clearer picture of your goals will illuminate the path forward. Our greatest glory is not in never falling, but in rising every time we fall.

Head Shepherd
P.O.G.
Loving Ministry

Mind
ADEQUATE

Never look to others for your sense of self-worth, self-esteem, self-belief, or self-love, as they ultimately must come from yourself. Use all the skills that you know you have deep down, and success will take care of itself. Self-love does not mean you're selfish. It means that you've finally learned what makes you happy and what your standards and boundaries are. You are a creation of the universal God. To obtain whatever you desire in life, you must first believe you can. Always strive to be better than the day before. Never stop reading and learning new things. When you are able to see yourself as the person God created you to be, then you will be in control of your destiny. Every single one of us is different and knows things that light us up and matter. Most of what matters to us is different. So rather than trying to shape our lives to look like someone else's or even like what we think others should like, we just have to choose. How you deal with them will only change your mind, not your circumstance. Gratitude, and abundance, is about overcoming the idea that when one thing is wrong everything is wrong, supporting all the things that are right, and realizing that you are enough, which creates a platform for joy and content. Then, you will want to progress out of love.

Head Shepherd
P.O.G.
Loving Ministry

Mind
ADVICE

P eople of God should be very approachable. People should not be afraid to talk to you. They should be able to see Christ's energy in us. We should put out a spirit of comfort and ability. Then people won't be afraid to approach us. There should never be a time when you can't listen to someone's concerns. Have an open heart and trust people. Listen to them first before you try to give them advice. Let them know why they are here. Tell them to surround themselves with people of holiness. Have them raise their expectations to overcome all life's circumstances, trust themselves, and listen to that little voice inside of them. Let God lead them through their trials and tribulations. When we can listen to the universal God, we will know exactly what we want to do in our lives. Let them know they're able to imagine. They can write their future. How much you are willing to learn is how much you rise up to be all you can be! Perception and intelligence are the key to life. Know yourself. We are all people who need others to truly be who God created us to be. We should listen with open hearts instead of closed minds. The art of openness requires us to remain vulnerable, transparent, and willing to trust again.

Head Shepherd
P.O.G.
Loving Ministry

Mind

AFRAID

....

What are you afraid of? Wow, that question can mean a lot of different things. Ask in a mocking tone, it can make us feel weak and helpless, increase our fear and doubt, drive us inward, and freeze us up. Ask genuinely and sincerely with compassion, it can give us courage to face what binds us. Help us name our fears, and free us to move forward. It's so easy to assume that Jesus took the more accusatory tone here, as though he was judging the disciples' lack of faith. But what if he really was inviting them to face what they feared, because they could draw courage from him? Our world creates a lot of shame around fear, teaching us to hide in it, bury it, or refuse to acknowledge it. But fear and doubt don't go away when we ignore them. They just sit inside, threatening to rear up and take us over. Naming what we fear is the most important step and takes away its power to dominate us. That can be hard to do especially when we feel alone. Jesus hears our fear without judging, and his resurrection gives us what we need to be free.

Head Shepherd
P.O.G.
Loving Ministry

Mind ANNOYING

When I was a child, my mother always seemed to know when I was going to do something – before I did. She would have my bath running when I came in the house from playing, because she knew I will be covered in mud. She knew how heartbroken I was when I lost a game, even when I tried to laugh it off and pretend I didn't care. She knew that my future wife would be my wife before I did. My mother, like any good parent, knew my heart, just as the Lord knows all the hearts of God's children. The disciples were praying for God's help in choosing who would take Judah's place amongst the disciples. They did not draw straws or ask for a show of hands. They asked God to look into their hearts and direct them to the right person to fill the position. Important decisions can be strenuous to make. They can stress us to the point of causing health problems. Or leading us to explode with anger. At such times it helps to remember that God knows our heart. God knows what we need. We can ask God for help and guidance and wait for the Lords reply.

Head Shepherd
P.O.G.
Loving Ministry

Mind
ANGER

A strong feeling of annoyance, displeasure, or hostility. When you are angry at someone, they can hear it in your voice. No matter how hard you try to be happy, they know you are not. When you are living with a negative emotion, it depletes you of who you are. Everybody gets angry from time to time, but when the degree of anger or aggression is greatly out of proportion to the situation, it's an indicator that something's wrong. When you get angry, you explode, and it generally lasts less than half an hour and can leave you feeling relieved but sometimes embarrassed by your words and actions. We need to try to stay positive to stay connected to the universal God's frequency. Anger is like a poison. It only hurts the soul. You need to stay filled with love and joy in order to have peace. You need to find your happy place. The essence of meditation practice is to make friends with our own minds and come home to the present moment. Over time, we can begin to understand and even be friends with ourselves as we are. Meditation is the perfect tool to get closer to our experience, and cultivate compassion, strength, and stability in our everyday lives. When you find yourself about to get angry, stop. Just breathe in, and out, close your eyes, and say, "God take this emotion away, in Jesus's name I pray." The greatest discovery of all time is that a person can change his life by merely changing their attitude.

Head Shepherd
P.O.G
Loving Ministry

Mind
APPRECIATE

Life isn't hard at all. It's all in how you look at it. If you believe life is hard, it will be. If you believe life is easy, it will be. The only thing that matters is what you believe. When you lack gratitude in your life, you always tend to complain, and have the worst outlook on things. Those who express their gratitude, and show their appreciation daily, are not only more of joy to be around, but are happier overall. Being grateful is more than a simple act. It is truly taking the time to appreciate parts of your life, including the people in it and what they do for you. Gratitude is truly an underrated emotion, but it can turn around your life. When your filled with gratitude, your entire mindset and outlook change. You become grateful for everything even if your situation isn't necessarily perfect. Even if you're in a difficult situation, gratitude can make you feel completely at ease. Gratitude is not an attitude. Gratitude is something that flows out of view when you are overwhelmed by the recognition of what you have received. Discipline is doing what you hate to do but nevertheless doing it like you love it. Success is a series of small endeavors that are repeated every day. Colossians 3:17 NIV, "And whatever you do, whether in word or deed, do it all in the name of the Lord Jesus, giving thanks to God the Father through him."

Head Shepherd
P.O.G
Loving Ministry

Mind
AWAKEN

Mark 14:37-38 NIV, "'Couldn't you keep watch for one hour? Watch and pray so that you will not fall into temptation.'" Good morning, my P.O.G. family Throughout the centuries, the Devil has been trying to rule the world. There have been countless wars of good against evil. He wants to keep the world in poverty, famine, and illiteracy so he can defeat those who believe. It is so hard for him, because he can only corrupt one man at a time to do his deeds. He has become the ruler of the air waves with this new technology. He has learned to use it to achieve his mission. There are seven continents in the world. If he is able to corrupt just one of them, he will be able to mobilize his demons. He would choose those who worship wealth, because he knows they thirst for more. Greed, arrogance, and selfishness are some of the tools he would use. He would give them dominion over the land to rule all the non- believers, let them be kings, and queens, and sit up on his crooked throne. They would use fear to deceive lots of people into believing that they know what is right for them to do. This world would become hell on earth. I know we like that feel-good ministry, but it is time to awaken. I am calling to arms all the believers to put on your full armor to drive back this force. We need all believers around the world to come together as one. To cry out to God to stop this beast from destroying humanity. AWAKEN AND SEE WHATS REALLY GOING ON.

Head Shepherd
P.O.G
Loving Ministry

Mind BEHIND

....

As we grow older, we begin to think about what we will leave behind for future generations. Do we have special jewelry to pass along? A journal filled with wisdom to impart? It is a real challenge to boil our lives down to their essence, to share with our descendants what matters to us. The next generation does listen to us. We just need to choose our words with care and speak our truth with convictions. The promise encourages the people of Israel of what the Lord has done for them and to pass that memory on to their children. God had done glorious things, and sharing those things will inspire faith in the next generations. We too, have a sacred responsibility to keep the story going from ages to ages so that the story of God's goodness is known to all God's children, and remembered far into the future.

Head Shepherd
P.O.G.
Loving Ministry

Mind
BEING MAD

Stop letting other people's opinions drive you mad. You are acting like a puppet by letting them pull your strings. People become angry when they perceive something as unpleasant, unfair, blameworthy, etc. There is always some sort of event that happens right before someone gets angry that serves as the trigger. Ultimately, whether we get angry and how we respond to a particular situation has to do with how we appraise or evaluate the situation. Whether you're angry about something that happened in the past, or something that's going on right now, learn to let it go, and forgive those that hurt you. Life is too short to walk around mad all the time. Be determined to keep your joy. No matter what you go through in life, remember it's just a bad day, not a bad life. Keep your joy! We all know what anger is, and we've all felt it, whether as fleeting annoyance or as full-fledged rage. Anger is a completely normal and usually healthy human emotion, but when it gets out of control and turns destructive, it can lead to problems at work, in your personal relationships, and with the overall quality of your life. Anger can make you feel as though you at the mercy of unpredictable and powerful emotions. You can't get rid of or avoid the things or people that enrage you, nor can you change them, but you can learn to control your reaction. "To do anything to high level it has to be total obsession."

Head Shepherd
P.O.G.
Loving Ministry

Mind
BELIEF

....

You can do anything as long as you have the passion and drive. With focus and support, your perception will become your reality in life. What you believe you will always achieve. Never let anyone else's opinion become your outcome in life. We as humans accumulate thousands of beliefs throughout our lifetimes about all aspects of life. We gain them through things that other people say to us—things we hear on the news, things we read, or any other external influences we are exposed to. Together with other factors, such as your personality, your genetics, and your habits, your belief system is one of the strongest forces that affects any decision you are making. The communication styles you use. The ways in which you react to anything that happens. Belief systems affect every area of your life. Beliefs affect most of your emotions, thoughts, productivity, relationships, and attitude. Mark 11:22-23 NIV, "'Have faith in God,' Jesus answered. 'Truly I tell you, if anyone says to this mountain, 'Go, throw yourself into the sea,' and does not doubt in their heart but believes that what they say will happen, it will be done for them.'" Incredible change happens in your life when you decide to take control of what you have power over instead of craving control over what you Don't.

Head Shepherd
P.O.G.
Loving Ministry

Mind

CALLING

A lot has changed in the world now from a year ago. You thought your calling was to be one thing, but now it's different. We are all called to have a purpose in life. To make a difference in someone's life. Be a person who serves humanity. We are called by God to make this world a peaceful place. Stop letting the problems of the world get to you and keep your peace. Whatever you do in life make sure it is making a difference in someone else's life. Be a giver not a taker, and always be willing to teach the importance of life. This gift-related calling is one that God places inside you before you are born and stays with you your entire life. It may manifest in different ways at different periods of your life, but it is always there. When and how it manifests depends on the skills and knowledge you have gained combined with your circumstances at any point. One time, it may be as simple as creating a friendship with another person. It may involve giving of your finances or skills. It may consist of investing your time to counsel or share your knowledge with other people. Whatever it is just do it with a happy heart. Knowing that you are making a difference in someone's life might be difficult, but the greatest satisfaction comes from helping others. The best life is a life devoted to the expression of qualities of virtue and passion that exhibit meaning in our lives.

Head Shepherd
P.O.G.
Loving Ministry

Mind
CHANCE

A set of circumstances that make it possible to do something. Mistakes are a part of life. It's your response to the error that counts. If you think that opportunities and rewards just fall into your lap by coasting on by, then you might be in for a surprise. Instead, you need to get off the couch, and find ways to attract opportunities. You need good habits that you can fall into and make a part of your daily routine that will get your name out there and make people aware of you. The more places your name floats around, then the more people are aware you exist, which leads to more opportunities being thrown your way! 1 John 4:1 NIV, "Dear friends, do not believe every spirit, but test the spirits to see whether they are from God, because many false prophets have gone out into the world." Don't let negativity disenchant you or your spirit. If you surround yourself with love and with the right people, anything is possible. The secret to success is to be ready when your opportunity comes. Opportunities to achieve what you want in life come to you more often than you realize. Most people live ready for what they expect in life and not what they want. Expectations lead to actions, which creates experience. However difficult life may seem, there is always something you can do and succeed at!

Head Shepherd
P.O.G.
Loving Ministry

Mind

CHALLENGE YOURSELF

Why is it hard for most of us to have what we want in life? I believe it's because we don't challenge ourselves. We are so quick to give up on our dreams. Any time the road is difficult to travel, we quit. There comes a time when you must go on, no matter what goes wrong. Life is never going to be easy to navigate. When the storms of life come and the boat begin to shake, that is when you must hold on. Change is coming. There will always be calm after the storm. Stay disciplined and focus to finish the race. Sometimes you have to make yourself do what's right in life. When times become uncertain, that is when you ask the Heavenly Father to show you the way. It may seem that you are at a dead end, but you must be able to make a way out of no way. God has given you the power of thought. When you tap into your mind, you become a creator. See yourself rising above all life problems. Tell yourself, "I am a champion. No weapon formed against me will ever prosper." Give God the glory. Knowing that He is your power, you are blessed and unstoppable. To become who you say you want to be, you have to practice what you preach. Challenge yourself every day to be consistent. Do what you love to make this your reality.

Head Shepherd
P.O.G.
Loving Ministry

Mind CHANGE

Years ago, Michael Jackson published the song "Man in the Mirror." The lyrics captured the idea that we can make the world a better place by being willing to change. In his letter to the Christians, Paul made the case that Jesus Christ is the image of the invisible God. He is the one through whom all things were created, and through whom all persons are reconciled. Christ is the head of the church, and the one we are called to emulate to follow a blameless life. Stand firm, Paul tells the Colossians, and remain steadfast. Martin Luther taught us to remember our baptism each day when we wash our face. This serves as a reminder that we too are created in the image of God and belong to Christ. The reflection we see in the mirror is the face of a child of God. We are meant to make the world a better place. As Luther taught, we are little Christs in the world!

Head Shepherd
P.O.G.
Loving Ministry

Mind
CHOOSE HAPPINESS

There is so much going on nowadays. The world is always changing and can get you upset about something. It's hard to keep your joy in this life. God has given you a spirit of happiness. Don't depend on people to make you happy in life. When you're ready to take control of your emotions, then you can take control of your life. Happy, or sad? How you think about a situation is in your hands. Just have a positive outlook. Use your energy to create a beautiful life. Tell yourself every day that good things are supposed to happen to you. You must be willing to do the things today others won't do in order to have the things tomorrow others won't have. Speak it into existence. Words are powerful and believe in your thoughts. So, think to be happy, and put it into action. One of the most important things you can learn is to control the words you speak. It's amazing how much negativity comes out of our mouth daily, and a lot of the time we don't even realize it. Happiness is a mindset. Wake up every morning with happiness on your mind. Go out in the world and let no one take your joy away that day. Then do this again each and every day. At that time, you're beginning to control your life. To accomplish great things, we must not only act, but also dream—not only plan, but also believe.

Head Shepherd
P.O.G.
Loving Ministry

Mind
CIRCUMSTANCE

I s better to be prepared for an opportunity than not to be. Whatever you want to do in life, you have to make preparations for it. Whenever you learn something new, you may think you're not going to need it, but the moment always comes when you do. Opportunities will always be there; you just have to be ready for them. A good mindset is very important to have when you're trying to make a choice. You must envision it first before achieving anything. Everything is easier when you have an opportunity to have it. Success is something you attract, not something you pursue. Control your thoughts and you control your life. You need to believe in yourself to achieve whatever you desire. It's not about what you do with your life, but how you live your life. Be a person of excellence and love those around you. Never take anyone for granted, because you never know what opportunity they may have for you. We need to always create thoughts of greatness in our minds. When you have a chance to make a difference in someone's life, you must always do it from your heart. God will tell you what to say or do in their life. Being a light of hope is what we must all seek. This world is so lost without us letting God guide us through it. We need one another's help in every way. It's time we started showing it to each other.

Head Shepherd
P.O.G.
Loving Ministry

Mind
CLARITY

....

The quality of being coherent and intelligible. Share your thoughts with others. Hear their thoughts. Just the act of talking it out is valuable. You're giving space for your thoughts and feelings and having them heard. Often you can get clarity from a good conversation. Living intentionally requires clarity. When you are clear about what makes you happy, healthy, loving, and wonderful, you can be happy, healthy, loving, and wonderful. Imagine a life with less confusion and doubt. Clarity makes everything easier, but getting there requires change and commitment, especially if you are busy, distracted, and overwhelmed. Your mind has to process everything that crosses your field of vision. You don't know what you don't know. Learn through experience and experiments. However, there comes a certain point when you just have to stop. You stop running through life and start looking around you, and ask yourself, "Am I on the right track? Am I on someone else track? Or am I just running this way, because it is the easiest way in life?" Many people make dozens of important life and business decisions without first considering what they want most. It's easy to waste time running in the wrong directions when you do not take time to evaluate where you want to go.

Head Shepherd
P.O.G.
Loving Ministry

Mind
COACH

....

Someone, somewhere, whose job it is to teach people to improve at a skill or subject. It's never the circumstance that determines success, but what you do with the current bad circumstances that determine your success in life. What makes for a great coach? It's the ability to lead to make things happen, maximize resources, and inspire. It's the extraordinary quality that solves problems and helps the individual come to a new level of understanding of what is possible. And it's the skill and talent to influence, and guide others to make real breakthroughs and create lasting change. Great coaches don't see things as worse than they are. They have a firm grasp on reality and are honest with themselves about where they stand unlike most people. However, they do not dwell on problems; they tackle them head on. They have the proper skills and knowledge to assess the situation and find the best path to move forward. Remember you can do anything you set your mind to, but it takes actions, persevering, and facing fears. To be a highly effective coach, it's a wise idea to choose a specific niche to focus on. The possibilities are endless. There are coaches who help people find love, and coaches who help business executives. Spiritual awareness creates more effective leaders. For your dreams to manifest, you need to be the first one that believes in you. Push yourself because no one else is going to do it for you. The best way to predict the future is to create it.

Head Shepherd
P.O.G.
Loving Ministry

Mind
COMFORT

A state of physical ease and freedom from pain or constraint. Sometimes you have to step out of your comfort zone to achieve what you want in life. It's said much is asked when much is given. You cannot be afraid to take risks in life. God did not give you a spirit of fear and doubt. The two most important days in your life are the day you are born and the day you find out why you were born. When you want to succeed as badly as you want to breathe, then you'll be successful. Life is full of opportunities to step outside your comfort zone, but grabbing hold of them can be difficult. Sometimes the problem is not being aware of the reason to do so. After all, if the feeling of comfort signifies our most basic needs are being met, why should we seek to abandon it? What holds people back most of the time is their frame of mind rather than any distinct lack of knowledge. Within their comfort zone, there isn't much incentive for people to reach new heights of performance. It's here that people go about their routine to avoid risks, causing their progress to plateau. When leaving their comfort zone, fear doesn't always equate to being in the panic zone. Fear can be a necessary step en route to the learning and growth zones. It takes courage to step from the comfort zone into the fear zone. Without a clear road map there's no way to build on previous experiences.

Head Shepherd
P.O.G.
Loving Ministry

Mind
COMPETE

....

Strive to gain or win something by defeating or establishing superiority over others who are trying to do the same. Never let the fear of striking out keep you from playing the game's perspective, and gratitude wins the game of life. In order to grow, we must go through different situations so that we may know the purpose of life. There have always been two different entities competing for the minds of humans. Everyone thinks they're competitive, but they aren't. They just like to win. They have no idea how to truly compete. Being a winner doesn't make you a competitor, but being a competitor will eventually make you a winner. Competitive people are simultaneously in a state of gratitude for how far they've come, and urge to do more, have more, and push further. Competing doesn't mean that you aren't happy with what you have. It only means that you have a deep understanding of an important universal truth. You're either getting better or you're getting worse. There are three types of people in this world: those in the game, those on the sidelines, and those in the stands watching. Which one of them are you in life? Get in the game. Win or lose, at least you tried! 1 Corinthians 10:31 NIV, "So whether you eat or drink or whatever you do, do it all for the glory of God."

Head Shepherd
P.O.G.
Loving Ministry

Mind
CONFIDENCE

Whenever you don't know something in life, don't be afraid to ask questions. There is no dumb question, just people afraid to have the knowledge. When you are confident about yourself, you are not worried about someone else's opinion. Be a person who meets others' needs. Whenever you do for others, you will always have what you need. When you know what you know, don't be afraid to speak out. All people like confident people on their team. Surround yourself with others who believe in what you believe. Whenever people are on the same page, that is when things began to happen. Be confident and take risks. You need to have faith in yourself. You don't have to have it all figured out to move forward. Ignore the negative people in your life. Just keep moving forward and never give up on prayer, no matter what. God will always be there for you. Your mindset is the key to everything in your life. When you focus on yourself, you will begin to understand life. Whatever you desire, it is all within your thoughts. Fight the good fight, and never give up! Negative self-talk makes us lose our purpose in life. Whenever we are able to keep God first in our lives, it will always turn out in our favor. When you're able to trust yourself, you will be able to create whatever reality you choose. God has given you the ability to do the impossible. Know yourself; then, you'll be able to love yourself.

Head Shepherd
P.O.G.
Loving Ministry

Mind
CONFLICT

A serious disagreement or argument, typically an instigated one. Believe in yourself. You are braver than you think, more talented than you know, and capable of more than you imagine. Conflict happens and is normal in relationships whether it's with a friend, roommate, or family member. Conflict can be uncomfortable and challenging for many of us, but there are ways to have difficult conversations and navigate disagreement with others. Here are some simple tips. How to stop conflict before it starts: When you have a disagreement with someone, what do you do? Do you tend to ignore the problem or avoid the person? Do you confront the person right away? Do you look for a compromise? Strengthening your relationships with others can help with preventing conflict. Communicating clearly can help prevent minor disagreements from becoming something bigger than they need to be. James 4:1-2, NIV: "What causes fights and quarrels among you? Don't they come from your desires that battle within you? You desire but do not have, so you kill. You covet, but you cannot get what you want, so you quarrel and fight. You do not have because you do not ask God." I don't believe you have to be better than everybody else. I believe you have to be better than you ever thought you could be.

Head Shepherd
P.O.G.
Loving Ministry

Mind
CREATE YOUR LIFE

....

Working hard is part of the training. It will help you to stronger and build your confidence. It will make you believe in yourself more. We all aspire to do, be and have great things, but most of us simply haven't created the successful life we want yet. We complain that we don't have enough money, romance, success, or joy in our lives. We point fingers and blame outsiders for problems that happen to us, making life more difficult. What we need to understand, and keep at the forefront of our minds, is that greatness exists in all of us. It is simply up to us to pull it out of ourselves. To live a life we can love, we can either love the one we already have, or change it to one we will. These two options may not be as difficult as they seem. In order to love the life we have, a change still needs to take place. We need to actively create changes in our livelihoods. Everyone has something they enjoy, and something they are good at. Sometimes it's simply hiding in plain sight. It doesn't seem like anything important somehow, but if you're good at it or enjoy it, whatever it is, it's important.

Head Shepherd
P.O.G.
Loving Ministry

Mind
DECEPTION

....

We all know someone (or several others) like this. Whether they're in our family, workplace, or worship community, there is often that one person who delights in speaking smoothly, but with an edge that sows dissent. But I want to call attention to those voices less noticeable, but just as troublesome. You see, character is catching. Children learn what they live; we all do. So, think today about how some news stories sensationalize personal violence and breed pervasive fear. Consider how some words, popular images of sex and violence, and heroes in movies might give us a distorted since of what seems normal. Realize that advertising can lure us into trusting the power of stuff to make us complete. We rarely take these voices personally, but they're around us all day long, often direct opposites to the teaching of our faith. Choosing to avoid them, or at least to intentionally limit their influence on our lives, isn't old-fashioned. It's part of the life we choose for ourselves, our children, and our communities.

Head Shepherd
P.O.G.
Loving Ministry

Mind

DECISION

....

When you focus on problems, you will have more problems. When you focus on the possibilities, you will have more opportunities. Whatever makes you the strongest, pursue that path. Adventure doesn't come if you sleep. You must get up and follow your heart; that is, aim to achieve your destiny. Decision-making is the process of making choices—identifying a decision, gathering information, and assessing alternative resolutions. Using a step-by-step decision-making process can help you organize relevant information and define alternatives. This approach increases the chances that you will choose the most satisfying alternative possible. Some people put off making decisions by endlessly searching for more information or getting other people to offer their recommendations. Intuition is a perfectly acceptable means of making a decision, although it is generally more appreciated when the decision is of a simple nature or needs to be made quickly. Decisions need to be capable of being implemented whether on a personal or an organizational level. Therefore, you need to be committed to the decision personally and be able to persuade others of its means. 2 Timothy 3:14 NIV, "But as for you, continue in what you have learned and have become convinced of, because you know those from whom you learned it." If you set your goals ridiculously high, and it's a failure, you will fail above everyone else's success.

Head Shepherd
P.O.G.
Loving Ministry

Mind
DESTINY

....

The hidden power believed to control what will happen in the future. We have the power over how our lives will turn out. From childhood, you have been told what you imagine yourself being and what will be your outcome in life. For as he thinks in his heart so is he. What people say with their mouths isn't what's in their hearts. When faced with this, which do you believe? You should believe what's in your heart. Your thoughts and the inclination of your heart shape the reality of who you are. They shape your thinking, which will ultimately shape your actions. Whatever you want to achieve in life, you must first believe it in your mind. Romans 12:2 NIV, "Do not conform to the pattern of this world, but be transformed by the renewing of your mind. Then you will be able to test and approve what God's will is—his good, pleasing and perfect will." We all have been given the gift by God to create whatever reality we choose. Your perception of life is how you will live it. Stop letting the enemy fill your head with negative thoughts. There is a power in you that will drive him back to the abyss that he is from. When you have truth on your side, there is no one that can defeat you. Your hardest times often lead to the greatest moments of your life. Tough situations build strong people. The only person you are destined to become is the person you decide to be!

Head Shepherd
P.O.G.
Loving Ministry

Mind DIFFICULTIES

If people are doubting how far you can go, go so far that you cannot hear them anymore. Start focusing on what you are doing instead of what other people are doing. No matter how badly someone treats you, never drop down to their level. Just walk away. Have you ever felt that your world is starting to fall apart because of how life tends to bombard you with seemingly impossible challenges? Reality has a way of reminding us that no matter how hard you try and how good you treat people, you will always have those days. Sometimes it's better to be alone and immerse yourself in the silence of solitude, not just to think but to refresh and recharge your mind from the noise of the outside world. This alone time can help you have a stress-free, and pressure-free, environment to just think and be with yourself. Everyone has difficulties. Dealing with them is how you overcome all your problems and become the best you in life. Someone's opinion of you does not have to become your reality. Believe in yourself. You are braver than you think, more talented than you know, and more capable than you can imagine.

Head Shepherd
P.O.G.
Loving Ministry

Mind

EDUCATE

....

To provide somebody with knowledge or training in a particular area or for a particular purpose. If you don't train this brain, it will use you instead of you using it. The distance between your dreams and reality is called action. Become the person you believe you were meant to be. Give intellectual, moral, and social instruction to someone, especially a child. Innovation and automation are in many industries of the world. It's a wonder watching them, but problems arise with more and more people being replaced with robots, and having to retrain or enter another field to do something that people are still doing. Most people often turn to go back to school rather than considering other options. While going back to school could be helpful, you can always consider learning how to educate yourself instead. Maybe a long time ago that option wasn't a reality, but with good quality information and other factors, educating yourself now is well worth considering. Even if you're not in the market for a new job, never stop learning. Your life depends on it, because learning is the way to have what you want. You learn how to challenge your mind and control your thoughts. Knowledge is the gatekeeper of life. Proverbs 12:1 NIV, "Whoever loves discipline loves knowledge, but whoever hates correction is stupid."

Head Shepherd
P.O.G.
Loving Ministry

Mind

EGO

Why do some people think they know it all? Always having an answer for everything, thinking others' opinions don't matter, going around just talking about themselves. You cannot tell them anything that is right. We need to stop letting them think they know it all. God has all the answers to everything. You need to listen to your heart. The heart is your connection to the divine Father. He knows what truly is in your heart. Stop thinking you have to have all the answers to every situation. You don't have to be in control of every aspect of your life. There comes a time when you have to listen to someone else besides your ego. The Father will never lead you in the wrong direction. Be that person who is willing to listen to someone besides yourself. God says when you're able to follow your heart, He will never depart from you. It's a great feeling when you know someone is standing there beside you. There's no greater joy knowing that God loves you. Ego can be destroyed by someone's words. God will never speak against you when He knows that you believe. Stop being of the world and be part of God's family. There is just peace and calmness when you surround yourself with true believers. There's power in His words. Listen, and then you will see!

Head Shepherd
P.O.G.
Loving Ministry

Mind
ENEMY

Exodus 23:22 NIV, "If you listen carefully to what he says and do all that I say, I will be an enemy to your enemies and will oppose those who oppose you."

Good morning, people of God. The devil knows the desires of your heart, so be careful of your thoughts. Even back in the days of the Bible, he knew that man could be tempted by a woman. That is why he had Eve tempt Adam to eat the apple. And when God found out that they had broken His Commandments, He kicked them out of the garden and told them that their descendants would be cursed for 6,000 years. That is why it is so easy for the devil to get inside of your head, because God is not there to protect you. You may think that no one knows your weakness like sex, alcohol, or drugs, but the enemy does. So, when he comes and begins to tempt you, just tell him, "Flee, you liar! You are not going to make me harm myself again, because I know my heavenly Father is greater than thee. So leave me, you liar, and in the name of Jesus I rebuke you!" You have the same power that your father had to resist your enemy. Believe in yourself and know that Jesus will never abandon you in your time of need.

Head Shepherd
P.O.G.
Loving Ministry

Mind
EXPERIENCE

Life isn't about finding yourself. It's about creating yourself. You will never have something different until you're willing to learn something new. The passion behind your goals is the experience. Better than what are you trying to accomplish is what you are trying to experience. Look around your physical environment. Is this the experience you want to have? What may initially seem crazy eventually becomes the most logical, clear explanation. The process of trusting your intuitive voice allows you to weave together inspired work and even an inspired life. Being fearless doesn't mean not feeling fear. We all feel fear. It means having control over that fear versus letting that fear control you. Being fearless forces you to be thoughtful around many aspects of your process and to be ready for obstacles that lie ahead. An engaged brain is a happy one. When you try new things, you give your brain a chance to come alive and get back in the game. Your brain loves let's-figure-this-out mode when you give it a chance. Proverbs 4:1-4 NIV, "Listen, my sons, to a father's instruction; pay attention and gain understanding. I give you sound learning, so do not forsake my teaching. For I too was a son to my father, still tender, and cherished by my mother. Then he taught me, and he said to me, 'Take hold of my words with all your heart; keep my commands, and you will live.'"

Head Shepherd
P.O.G.
Loving Ministry

Mind
EXPERT

A person who has comprehensive and authoritative knowledge of a skill in a particular area. An expert is someone that is good at what they do, but often, when it comes to believing, they fall short. During the past year, we had all types of experts telling us how to live our lives, but in the end, some of them were very wrong. It goes to say, be very careful who you listen to. People spend years in school studying to be better at what they do. Why can't you do the same with the word? God has given us the blueprint on how to create the reality we choose. It costs us nothing more than some time and the right attitude. No one has all the answers, but God has a way to show you how to be a good leader. The price for this is to meditate and pray for clarity. To be the best at what you do, try treating others with love. Your mind will manifest whatever your thoughts are. Stay filled with the possibility to change your reality. When you're connected to God then you will know your purpose in life. You will begin to help others with the skill you have. Money will no longer be a problem because God will take care of your needs. People will begin to gravitate towards you. They will listen to everything you tell them in Jesus's name. Every situation in life you face will turn out in your favor. Only then you will be a true leader.

Head Shepherd
P.O.G.
Loving Ministry

Mind
FLEXIBILITY

Willing to change or compromise is how P.O.G. needs to be in every situation. There is no one way of seeing things. There is this old saying: "There's more than one way to scan a cat." You cannot let your ego lead you to think that everything you say or do is right. If we as people could learn to listen, this world would be a much better place. As people, we must learn to adapt. When our environment in this world changes, stop thinking that you are only capable of doing one thing. There are a variety of things you can do in this world. When you believe in your ability, your mind is one of the most powerful computers in the world. When you program it right, you can accomplish any task. Flexibility is an important skill to master, whether it means having the ability to overcome stress or simply to adjust to change quickly. Having a high level of flexibility makes it easier for you to live a less stressful and less hectic life. Everything is easier when you don't concern yourself with what other people are doing. The past and the future do not matter. It is the here and now that will impact your life and how it will turn out. Everything you do brings you closer to your desire or your imaginal act. You get what you think about in life. Also, take quality time out every day for the special people in your life.

Head Shepherd
P.O.G.
Loving Ministry

Mind
FREE

....

Paul reminds us in Romans six and seven whoever has died is free from sin. We are free and alive in Christ Jesus. So, to use the words of Martin Luther, what does this mean for us today? "We are alive! We are no longer weighed down by sin and the power of death. Our heavy burdens have been removed. Our chains of doubt have been broken. We live in confidence that God loves us unconditionally and forever. Like the butterfly who breaks out of the restrictive cocoon and flies freely you and I are free" to do what? Fill in the blank: free to share good news, free to help a stranger and visit those who are in prison, or free to work for justice and peace in the world. Consider anew that you are alive to God and Christ Jesus. How will you live?

Head Shepherd
P.O.G.
Loving Ministry

Mind
FREE TO BE YOU

How many of you live your lives doing what you like? Not punching in to the time clock or having someone telling you what to do. Just living life how you choose to. We are all creators who build the reality we want. We all have a gift inside of us that will take care of us. Don't be afraid to step out on faith. Pray and believe in your ability to be free. Wouldn't it be great to live life carefree, without a worry in the world? Living every day doing what you want to do. Coming and going as you choose with no one telling you what to do. You are in control of your destiny, so go on whatever journey inspires you. Could you imagine living your dream? The reason that we ever lack freedom is because we have attached ourselves to a certain belief—a belief that is probably not true but has stuck with us. Maybe we don't feel that we are good enough. We don't feel that we are good looking enough, or maybe we don't feel like we are worthy enough. Well, as long as we keep telling ourselves that, we will never be free. Remember: live for today, forget about yesterday, and let tomorrow worry about itself. Be free like a bird out of its cage. Fly to where you want to explore. Stop letting the enemy keep you chained down to its negative thoughts. Free yourself and live life to its full potential.

Head Shepherd
P.O.G.
Loving Ministry

Mind FREQUENCY!

We all have receptors somewhat like antennas that keep us connected with God. Your mind and your thoughts are how you communicate with God. He hears everything that you think, so it's important to have positive thoughts. When you're able to have a pure heart, your thoughts are clean. Have you ever heard cleanliness is next to godliness? Your soul is immortal; it lives forever. Look at it this way: When your television doesn't work, and you go out to buy a new one, you are transmitting the same frequency to the new one. You are raw energy in human form. There is no limit to your power to accomplish anything. You can say, "Mountain, move," and it will when you believe. When you believe, there are no limits to what you can do; the sky is the limit. Faith without action is dead. You need to start doing what you say. With the right belief, you can manifest the reality you want in life. Your DNA is the same of the Almighty God. We are all creators of our environment. We have to stay positive about life knowing it will always work out. Even if bad times come, we will get through them with God's love. We are made in the image of God. We are divine, so we must operate not in the survival of the fittest, but in a way that supports everyone and everything in this world.

Head Shepherd
P.O.G.
Loving Ministry

Mind
FULFILLMENT

The elevator to success is out of order. You'll have to use the stairs one step at a time. Don't limit yourself. Many people limit themselves to what they think they can do. You can go as far as your mind lets you. Remember: What you believe you can achieve. What you do makes a difference, and you have to decide what kind of difference you want to make. As humans, we all want to feel fulfilled. We want to live life feeling happy and satisfied with what we have accomplished. This feeling is not always easy to come by, though, which can lead some people to feel depressed or hopeless about their future. To feel satisfied, it's important to take an honest stock of all the different things in your life and how they make you feel. You need to think about everything that makes you happy or gives you meaning or a sense of completion. This includes relationships, hobbies, feeling like you're making a difference in the world, feeling loved, and feeling appreciated. This also includes feeling fulfilled with your career or academic life. When we live out our purpose of loving, caring, and sharing with each other, then you will feel fulfilled. We must stop living for ourselves and start helping one another. Galatians 5:14 NIV, "For the entire law is fulfilled in keeping this one command: 'Love your neighbor as yourself.'"

Head Shepherd
P.O.G.
Loving Ministry

Mind
FUTURE

As long as you keep on fighting, and giving your best every single day, you will win. One of the biggest advocates of the notion that your past does not equal your future is your future itself. Building a great future will require making changes to your life now. The things you do today will affect your tomorrow. You must live in the moment to make your future bright. Be happy in every minute. Stop worrying about tomorrow and let this moment prepare you for it. The good news is you can create your own future by believing in yourself and letting God in. Don't leave your future to chance, luck, or the whims of others. Instead, unlock, and live your best future, beginning in the here and now. Don't let a lack of confidence stop you from trying something new. Get more information, seek guidance, and take one step forward, then another. With each step in the direction of your goal, your confidence will grow. It is so easy to be overwhelmed by despair or fear in the world today. SIN, war, cancer, and sickness all find a way to steal our hope and cause us to doubt that there is a good future ahead. Yet God promises us that he plans a good, hopeful future for us. Through the power of the Holy Spirit, you are able to look forward with joy to God's destiny. Your happiness depends upon the quality of your thoughts. Therefore, guard accordingly and take care that you entertain no notions unsustainable to virtue and responsible nature.

Head Shepherd
P.O.G.
Loving Ministry

Mind
GIVING AND RECEIVING

We all have been on the receiving end of getting things. It momentarily makes us feel good about ourselves, but giving is much different. Why is that? People are so selfish, feeling that they don't want to share any of the abundance that they have. There are many benefits to being generous. Generosity is good for your psychological well-being, your relationships, and possibly even your physical health. But the truth is that some people have more generous dispositions than others. For some of us generosity just doesn't come as easily. I think that it is because you haven't been taught the art of giving. We are all like magnets. What you put out in the universe is what you will attract back. If you want good things to happen to you, do good things for others. You have probably heard the familiar adage, "It is better to give than to receive." It would be difficult to find someone who would say otherwise. The act of giving elicits positive feelings and emotions for both the giver and the receiver, making it one of the most important exchanges you can have with someone. The action of giving and receiving has a powerful impact on a relationship not only with others but with yourself as well. Think about your past experiences with giving and receiving. After some consideration, you may realize that you are better at one than the other. Some people want it to happen, some wish it would happen, and others make it happen.

Head Shepherd
P.O.G.
Loving Ministry

Mind
GOALS

....

What we want to achieve is much more meaningful than just what we need to accomplish to survive. Unlike daily routines or short-term objectives, our goals drive our behavior in the long run. We all need some type of system in place for us to have what we desire. It is said that a person who fails to plan is a person who plans to fail. Whatever you want to be in life, you must first envision yourself becoming it. Write it down; speak about it as much as you can; tell others, "This shall be mine, because God has said." Many people feel as if they are adrift in the world. They work hard, but they don't seem to get anywhere worthwhile. A key reason that they feel this way is that they haven't spent enough time thinking about what they want from life and haven't given themselves formal goals. Would you set out on a major journey with no destination? Probably not. When you allow things to bother you, you are giving them power over you. Keep your positive attitude and keep moving forward. That's where the real power is prayer. You create your thoughts, your thoughts create your intention, and your intention creates your reality. Keep reminding yourself of the big picture. Remind yourself the reason why you started. Focus on yourself before you focus on your dreams.

Head Shepherd
P.O.G.
Loving Ministry

Mind

HELP

Leviticus 25:35, NIV, "If any of your fellow Israelites become poor and are unable to support themselves among you, help them as you would a foreigner and stranger, so they can continue to live among you."

Do you find it difficult to ask people for help? You fear that they may use it against you, or you are simply too proud. My husband always says a closed mouth never gets fed. No one is useless in this world who lightens the burdens of another. The best way not to feel hopeless is to get up and do something. There is no exercise better for your heart than reaching down and lifting people up. My P.O.G. family, we have to start helping and uplifting one another. That is the best way to fight the devil. If we show him how much we love, care, and share with one another, he will not win. We can claim the victory. Remember this: "I will love the light for it shows me the way, yet I will endure the darkness, because it shows me the stars." The best preparation for tomorrow is doing your best today. The best and most beautiful things in the world cannot be seen or even touched they must be felt with the heart. Help one another.

Lady Shepherd
P.O.G.
Loving Ministry

Mind
HELPING!

....

From the beginning of time, we were asked to help one another. We all are able to do something special with our own lives. You have a unique talent to create things. Some are builders, farmers, or healers. God has given us all a gift to share with others. We are here for a reason, and that is to help someone. When we can stop our own selfish ways, then we will be living in our powers. Be a person who uplifts others to their full potential. Some have more than others, so be willing to share with them. When you give, God said you will not need. What you put out in the universe, you will attract back. Help someone so you can help yourself. If we all just start helping one another, there will be no need for government assistance. With all the different talents people have, we can create the reality we want. Mother Earth has all the resources we need. There's water, soil, and fire; that is a good start. The trees are the lumber we need for shelter. The enemy has deceived us in believing we need all these materialistic things to survive. When you live your life doing for others it will make you feel good about yourself. God said, "When you help the least of thee, he will always provide for what you need." You can help others in so many ways, like teaching, listening, or giving some good advice. There are so many different cultures in this world. We all have something to offer one another. It's time to stop loving things, and start loving others. Whenever you help with an open heart, you're creating a better world.

Head Shepherd
P.O.G.
Loving Ministry

Mind
IGNORANCE

From birth, we do what we are told by those in authority. God said if you don't seek truth, you will stay ignorant. The enemy will keep you enslaved in Misery. We all have eyes and ears, yet we believe what the master of the airwaves tell us. We have all become selfish, arrogant, and too lazy to do our own research. You need to know what the enemy has in store for you. It is not something that you will enjoy. We have been programmed to believe that materialistic things are what we should seek, and not self-knowledge. The religions that you follow have been twisted to deceive you to make you follow the ways of the evil one. We have the power to change the course of history. We can't just get sit back and do nothing. Stop buying into all of this propaganda and fear. Start believing in who you really are—a person of great spiritual powers. Don't let this enemy have authority over you, because you are the one who has power over him. There is power in the name, so use it to transform this world. We must all believe the impossible is possible, especially when we all are on the same frequency of love. If you are not doing something about the problem, then you are part of the problem. Take the muzzle off your face and speak out about the injustice of the world. We are not going to be a human bar code. Unite, because love is the only thing that can turn the world back to sanity. Be yourself and stop trying to be of the world. When you're able to love yourself, the world will be a happier place.

Head Shepherd
P.O.G.
Loving Ministry

Mind
IMAGINE

Look at things that could be and ask, why not? Imagine the world free from worry, sorrow, and pain. People showing love and compassion to one another. Mother Earth has no toxin or disease in the land. When we are all able to focus as one then this shall be possible. We are all connected to God with our thoughts. It gives us the ability to communicate with the Father. Can you imagine that you're able to have a one-on-one with him? Ask for what you want your reality to be. When we live our lives doing for others it will make this world a better place. Your words are power; speak them over your loved ones. When you do the will of God, there is more peace, joy, and happiness in life. You must shift your attitude to I can, I will, do this. To enjoy the benefits of God you have to be disciplined. Be consistent in everything you do in life. People must be able to see that you believe in Christ. When we all know our purpose, then we begin to create a new life. Imagine a world filled with empathy for others. The lion will be able to lay down with the sheep. There will be no more color just love for one another. Always feel you have worth. Your life has a purpose. If you live the life which you have imagined, you will meet with unexpected success. You must envision yourself doing what you have decided to do!

Head Shepherd
P.O.G.
Loving Ministry

Mind
IMPACT

....

The one mistake we make in life is believing we have time. Find your purpose in life when hard times come. It will help you push forward. Perhaps the most powerful influence in our lives comes from the relationships we pursue. They influence our thinking, attitude, and views. And these same relationships give us the opportunity to positively make an impact on lives of others. However, making an impact on another starts with you and your life. You see people watch you in ways you're not even aware of. Because of this, how you live your life will have the greatest impact on others. To do something you've never done, you must be someone you've never been. We want to find meaning in our lives. Give back and learn how to make an impact on others. Provide that meaning because it makes life about something much larger than ourselves. It fulfills our essential human needs to feel significant and to contribute. When we help others, we grow in our personal lives and make progress towards unlocking an extraordinary life. We break out of our limiting beliefs about how much good one person can actually do in the world and see firsthand that even the smallest acts of kindness can transform lives. Do what you can where you are with what you have.

Head Shepherd
P.O.G.
Loving Ministry

Mind
INSTINCTS

Have you ever had a thought in your head? Knowing that something is supposed to happen in your life? The feelings were so strong, yet you let the dark forces drive them away. Why is it that it's so hard for people to follow their instincts? When you are connected to the universal God, he will always send clear signals. Focusing on ourselves is a valid way to bloom in our own life. If we know what our own personal values are and prioritize them, people can come and go from our lives without disrupting our sense of self. When you can think through the decisions in your life, they will always turn out right. The most important skill in the world is to control your mindset, because it controls your actions. You sense that something isn't right even though you can't explain why. Call it your gut, say it's your instinct, but ultimately it's a subtle sense of knowing. Some folks try to explain it using thoughts or facts, but often it's just something you feel. Now, how often you feel it and then ignore it? Your inner voice is talking to you, but you're not listening, because it doesn't make sense. Most of us recognize that our inner voice has value. That is when God is communicating with you. The problem is we have no idea how to tune in to God. How to hear him and listen. Most of the time, the problem is that we're just not paying attention. Of course, it's incredibly difficult to listen to a voice that's not telling you what you want to hear. Trust God, because he will never lead you wrong!

Head Shepherd
P.O.G.
Loving Ministry

Mind
IT'S IN YOU!

Whatever you want in life, you must first believe it will happen for you. We have been dependent on man for so long to tell us how to live our lives. Christ is with you in your heart, so free it. You have been given the power to create your reality. The thoughts of people determine how the world will be. Have positive thoughts and believe in a beautiful world. We pray and hope but never take action to change this world. It's up to us, not Christ, to come down and save us. Your Christ conscience is what will save you. Stop being of the world and start changing it for the better. The enemy for centuries has been programming us to do his will. God gave us free will to choose from right or wrong. We have the authority over our lives. You just have to know what you want from life. We are the true people of this world; it's up to us to start acting like it and stop being scared to take charge over our lives. Walk and talk like someone of importance. God has placed something wonderful in our DNA. We are He and He is we. Whatever your perception of life is, that will be your reality. God has given you dominion over the land. Other people's opinions should never stop you from living out God's Commandments. When you listen to your heart, that is the universal God leading you to the path of righteousness. Be not of the world, but be who God created you to be—someone with morals and convictions about life.

Head Shepherd
P.O.G.
Loving Ministry

Mind
KARMA

The cycle of cause-and-effect. What happens to a person happens because they caused it with their actions. Whatever thought you send out to the universe will always come back to you. That is why you have to say words of encouragement over your life and others. Be not deceived; God is not mocked. "What soever a person soweth that shall they also reap." It is vital that you live a righteous life. If you want to change the way you live your life, change the way you perceive it. There comes a time when we must break the generational curse over our families. Stop being of the world and have standards over your life. No matter what you're going through, you must believe you can rise above it. If you don't pass the test in this life, you will repeat it in the next life. We must do what God says to be able to move to the next dimension. Just treat others with love, respect, and compassion. Keep hate and envy, out of your heart. Be filled with positive energy. Live life as a new, exciting adventure every day. Be filled with the Holy Spirit when you speak about others. Don't let others' opinions sway you from your walk with Christ. Stand strong in His words so others can see you as a beacon of light. Be willing to give to all those in need. When you're able to do these things you will be on your way to meet the Father.

Head Shepherd
P.O.G.
Loving Ministry

Mind

KEEP ENCOURAGED MY SISTAHS!

1 Thessalonians 5:11, NIV, "Therefore encourage one another and build each other up, just as in fact you are doing."

Every day, we experience so many different situations where we are reminded that we are people of color. It just so shocking how we experience racism on such a level that is hidden, yet so blatantly in your face. The media portrays us to be promiscuous, having a bad attitude, not supportive of our men, superficial, lazy, and a mean-spirited group of people. It is so sad to have that type of persona when you have not demonstrated that type of personality at all. I hate that we are not valued in the workplace or in society. The other day at work, we were discussing a problem with a security issue that we have been bringing up for years. We even came up with a solution to the problem. However, when this individual encountered something we all feared would happen, it was taken care of right away. It was so ironic that all my brown sistahs felt the same way, but we were slighted and ignored. This is just one example; there are several. But I want to tell my brown sistahs to keep your heads up. Do not perpetuate the stereotype. Keep educating and seeking knowledge. We are unique, and we age well. Just remember greatness is not measured by what a man or woman accomplishes, but by the opposition he or she has overcome to reach their goals. Keep moving.

Lady Shepherd
P.O.G
Loving Ministry

Mind

KINDNESS

Galatians 5:22 NIV, "But the fruit of the Spirit is love, joy, peace, forbearance, kindness goodness, faithfulness."

Good morning, my P.O.G. family. Have you ever thought that the word kindness would be a foreign word in today's society? I mean, we had a president who promotes hatred to other groups of people. I never thought that I would be too afraid to approach a stranger to say good morning or to see an elderly person and ask if I can hold the door for them. I am hesitant because of the reaction I may get. But at the end of the day that does not stop me from trying to do small acts of kindness towards others. That is the way I was taught to behave. Some things never leave you. Kindness is like igniting a light in someone else for no reason other than to watch them enjoy the glow. Kindness is giving hope to those who think they are all alone in this world. No matter what people tell you, words and ideas can change the world.

Lady Shepherd
P.O.G.
Loving Ministry

Mind
BASIC KNOWLEDGE

As people of God, we need to know the basic things we need to be doing. The way we have been taught is not the way God want us to live. The enemy has so much control over our lives. We need to learn that love has true power. Choose love over everything in your life. Fear is just the tool the enemy uses to keep you in check. We all need to care for each other. Knowledge only works when you know how to use it. If you know something, and you are not doing something about it, than it is dead. God said faith without action is dead. God's words are the right way to live our life. We need to learn how to take care of our mental health so we can live right. We are all connected. We need to be around each other and not be afraid to connect. Our power is at its greatest when we are united. That is why it is important to love your kids unconditionally so they will know their power. That is why the Ancient One said it takes a village to raise a child. Your belief system is the healing for your body. No matter what tries to take it over, your beliefs will heal your body. The power is in his words. That is why you must use words of encouragement. Stay filled with good energy. Be happy and joyful about your life. These are the secrets of the universe that we should all know. Let your heart guide you, and then you will be all right.

Head Shepherd
P.O.G.
Loving Ministry

Mind
KNOWLEDGE

....

When I was in school, I did pretty well in my classes. I was the first one in my family to go to college. But I'm glad there are people who are a lot smarter than I am. I give thanks that I do not have to rely on my intelligence alone to get through life. Every day, new discoveries are made, things are invented, and knowledge is added to our existence. It seem there is no end to the imagination and capacity of the human mind, yet no matter how much we think we know, there is still so much more we cannot comprehend. We are wise to own up to our limitations. Even really intelligent people can do really stupid things. I'm humbled by the fact that I can learn from my child. I am humbled that my smartphone knows more than I do. I am humbled – and thankful – that the foolishness of God's love in Jesus Christ is greater than human wisdom. And God's weakness is stronger than human strength. How reassuring that He knows more and loves more than we ever will.

Head Shepherd
P.O.G.
Loving Ministry

Mind LIMITATIONS

Whenever you speak negatively about your life, you limit your expectations. To have no limits, your thoughts must be of possibilities. Whatever you desire in life, you must envision it all the time. The mind is for us to program how we see our life. Thoughts are the foundation to be able to create your reality. Your words are your reality. Your life will move in the direction of your words. The first thing you have to do is become conscious of you subconscious thoughts. Once you replace your negative thoughts with positive ones, life will be all right. Success has to happen inside your mind first before you can manifest in your life. Once you achieve something that you thought was impossible, all things will become possible. Success is not about your resource, but the belief in yourself. Unleash the inner you to be that person you were created to be. Have self-awareness and listen to that positive voice inside of you. You become what you think about all day long. Be one with God and let God be everything in your life. You must be convinced that no limitation will stop you from achieving what you desire in life. Stop waiting around for something to happen. Go out and make it happen. There are no limits to what you can do with your life. God has said you can do all things when you believe in the Son. Understand you must have the faith to get what you want in life.

Head Shepherd
P.O.G.
Loving Ministry

Mind
LIVE, LOVE, LAUGH

Live, love, and laugh. No matter what the world throws your way, live life to the fullest. When we can enjoy every moment in life, then you are living. Don't worry about what people may think of you. Just know Jesus loves you. Wake up every day with a smile on your face. With positive energy, we are able to make this world a beautiful place. Do not let evil control your thoughts. Live life expecting everything to come your way. Be bold and courageous. Speak whatever you decide into existence. Love yourself first; then, reach out and love others. God has placed unconditional love in your heart, so make sure that you follow this principle. Love is one of the most powerful emotions in the universe. The Bible says God so loved the world that he gave his only begotten son, so that you shall have everlasting life. There's no one on this planet that does not need love. Have compassion and empathy for all humanity. Love is the solution to change the world from dark to light. We must learn to laugh at ourselves when we make mistakes in life. Laughter is the best medicine for the soul. When we laugh the whole world laughs back. Stop being so uptight about life, and learn to relax, and have a piece of mind. You are worthy of anything you desire. Success isn't created by accident, but by design. You have a creative mind and an unlimited potential. Never forget it is never too late to laugh and be happy.

Head Shepherd
P.O.G.
Loving Ministry

Mind MAGNET

....

The most important words to tell yourself are, "I believe in me." You have to be your biggest cheerleader. The greatest glory lies not in falling, but in rising every time we fall. Your thoughts will attract what you want your life to be. We are like magnets we attract our reality in life. Learn how to be happy with what you have while you pursue all that you want. The law of attraction says that what you think about is what you attract into your life. When we surround ourselves with great people, we are much more likely to do great things. The truth is we need people. No one person is an island. Association is so important to the way we think and act. Surround yourself with amazing people who are in the pursuit of worthwhile dreams and goals. If you want to attract other amazing people to you, then be amazing too. Be what you want. We are drawn to those who are like minded. Be the person that builds people up, not one who tries to tear people down. Speak what you want. Positive self-talk can give you the power and focus that you might not otherwise have. Limit your time with people who drain your energy. Get good at communicating your vision with others. Make the invisible clearly visible to them through your excitement and words. Paint a picture of what you see so that others can learn how they can be a part of it. The world will change its opinion about you the day you do!

Head Shepherd
P.O.G.
Loving Ministry

Mind
MENTORSHIP

A mentor may share key information with you about his or her own career path as well as provide guidance, motivation, emotional support, and role modeling. A mentor may help with exploring careers, setting goals, developing contacts, and identifying resources. We all need to be willing to help young people become leaders. We have left it up to social media and the media to raise our children. It is time we get involved into their life. To help them make the right decisions. Stop letting others indoctrinate them to their agenda. Show them how to become outstanding human beings. Instill character and value into their lives. Be a teacher to others, always giving hope to them. Show love and compassion to one another. Let the children of the world know they can achieve their dreams. Never give up on someone who is trying to change their life. Be that coach that always encourages someone. Lead by example, always doing what is right. Don't ever let the worldview change your character. God will always stand beside you when you are true to yourself. Tell people they can accomplish all things when they believe in themselves. We all need to be strong and courageous, and not let life's disappointments stop us from moving on. Everyone needs someone to help them carry on in life. Tell them not to be afraid to seek the path of righteousness in life. When you are able to walk in faith, you begin to build confidence in your life. Be that coach to others, always showing them what's right. Tell them how great they are and that all things are possible with Christ. When we are able to show others about the salvation of Christ, then we will be living a wonderful life.

Head Shepherd
P.O.G.
Loving Ministry

Mind
MOVE ON

It is so hard to do something else when you already have it in your mind to do this one thing. People don't realize that you get stuck if you don't have the ability to move on. We look for happiness in all the wrong places. We have to give God a chance to do something good in our lives. Stop blocking your blessings, and be still, and listen to what God has in store for you. Sometimes in life you have to close some doors not because of pride, incapacity, or arrogance, but simply because they no longer lead somewhere. I know the unknown is scary but, if you trust in God, He will grant your request. It took me fourteen years to realize that. You should never be a victim of your circumstance. Even if you don't have the support of your family, you have to remember to always rely on God. He will lead you in the right direction. You will know right away because you decision will become so peaceful. You don't deliberate in your head, heart, or spirit when you consult the Lord. Just remember you can't get back time. I just wish that someone would have educated me at a young age how important it is to have a relationship with God. Proverbs 3:5-6 NIV, "Trust in the LORD with all your heart, and lean not on your own understanding; in all your ways submit to him, and he will make your paths straight."

Lady Shepherd
P.O.G.
Loving Ministry

Mind MULTIPLIER

Don't depend on other people to change you. The power is within all of us. We must hold ourselves responsible, and take action every single day to make things happen. Be thankful for what you have. You'll end up having more. If you concentrate on what you don't have, then you will never have enough. You need to take every good thing in life and multiply by two; then, you will have more. Never stop developing yourself to be better. Genesis 22:17 NIV, "I will surely bless you and make your descendants as numerous as the stars in the sky and as the sand on the seashore. Your descendants will take possession of the cities of their enemies." I am on a journey to reprogram my whole life, and to spread joy and love to those around me! If you believe in yourself, have dedication and pride, and never quit, you'll be a winner. The price of victory is high, but so are the rewards. If you want to multiply what you have, the way we live together makes us human. Mutual respect, and friendly interaction make us good people. It is an incredibly great feeling to share your happiness with other people. You don't have to know them. You don't have to pay a price for it. You just do something good. I try to integrate this happiness into my everyday life in such a way that others can also profit from it.

Head Shepherd
P.O.G.
Loving Ministry

Mind NAVIGATION

The road to happiness in life is sometimes hard to navigate around. It seems like we're always coming to a dead end with no way to turn! The people in our lives have given up on us and stopped giving us any encouragement to carry on. We must see the big picture to understand our purpose in life. Face the fear and do it anyway. Life is never perfect; it's what you make it. Stop letting people block you from doing what you want. Become a master of your craft; whatever you want to do, go after it with all your heart. There will always be obstacles in life that you will have to go around. You must believe that you can do what it takes. To have what you want in your reality, you don't know how much time you have. It's time to start living your life. However you spend your time, it tells you who you are. Be that person who is always thriving to be the best. When you're able to let your actions speak for you, then you know you're on the way to success in your life. Confuse them with silence but show them with your actions. Then they will know you are person of excellence. God will always help a child who helped themselves.

Head Shepherd
P.O.G.
Loving Ministry

Mind
NEGATIVE THINKING

If you don't know who you truly are, you'll never know what you really want. You have to learn to deal with negative thoughts and stop putting them off. Negative or positive, good or bad, are all the same in our universe. Don't limit yourself. Many people limit themselves to what they think they can do. You can go as far as your mind lets you. Remember, what you believe, you can achieve. Many people whose lives seem to have spiraled out of control have no idea how to climb out of the pit of despair they find themselves in. They may feel that everything seems to go wrong, and their situation gets worse and worse. When they don't get the results they want, they give up and resign to a life of strife and unhappiness. Become aware of how your thoughts are impacting your emotions and observe your behaviors and thoughts. Ask yourself if this thought is helpful. What purpose is the thought serving you? How does the thought make you feel? Start focusing on positive things in your life. Try to shift your focus and see yourself being happy again. This can go a long way to helping you overcome your negative thinking. The more you shift the focus of your mentality to positive things in your life, the easier it is going to be for you to think and act positively.

Head Shepherd
P.O.G.
Loving Ministry

Mind
OBSTACLE

A thing that blocks your way or prevents or hinders progress. You don't get what you want in life; you get what you are. It's never too late to change your life for the better. You don't have to take huge steps to change. Making even the smallest change to your daily routine can make a big difference. Don't let yesterday take up too much of today. Like everything in the universe, we are connected to a sea of information in a dimension beyond space, and time. To be successful you must be able, at any moment, to sacrifice what you are for who you will become. Appreciate obstacles; they serve a purpose other than cause emotional distress. To contest reality will not earn you support since life always prevails. However, learning from your challenges helps you move through the obstacles rather than allow them to dominate your life. By learning from your challenges, you embrace life through your nonresistance. The obstacle reveals vital lessons to identify its significance. Be willing to leave behind pursuits that do not deliver results. Far too many people discount the value of redirecting their attention when all the attempts are exhausted. Pride, self-worth, and time investment are the main reasons most people don't move ahead in life.

Head Shepherd
P.O.G.
Loving Ministry

Mind
OPENNESS

The best day of your life is the one when you decide your life is your own. No apologies or excuses. No one to lean on, rely on, or blame. The gift is yours. It is an amazing journey. Be open to new things. The two most important days of your life are the day you were born and the day you discover why! In many ways, we close ourselves off to life in all its fullness. We close ourselves off to others as a form of self-defense. It happens to all of us. When you left yourself open in the early part of your life, you likely would get hurt from time to time. That pain taught us to close ourselves off in different ways – not to let others in, use humor to keep some distance, hurt others before they hurt you, back away from anything new, and so on. What does it mean to be open? It means that you accept life without judgment and are happy no matter what comes. It means you judge other less, criticize less, accept others more, and learn more about their wonderful particularity. It means more than ever before. You are fully experiencing life. We take things personally too often. If you could truly see that what other people do and say is a reflection of what's happening inside of them, you would process your feelings, wish them well from afar, and move on. 2 Timothy 2:15 NIV, "Do your best to present yourself to God as one approved, a worker who does not need to be ashamed and who correctly handles the word of truth."

Head Shepherd
P.O.G.
Loving Ministry

Mind
OPPORTUNITIES

Sometimes you have to go through something to find out who you really are. The longer it takes, the better it's going to be. Walk by faith not by sight. When you know what you want in life, no one can stop you from having it. God has placed a power in you to defeat all darkness around you. If you think that opportunities and rewards just fall into your lap by coasting on by, then you might be in for a surprise. Instead, you need to get off the couch, and find ways to attract opportunities. You need good habits that you can fall into and make a part of your daily routine that will get your name out there and make people aware of you. The more places your name floats around, then the more people are aware you exist, which leads to more opportunities being thrown your way! Good things don't usually just fall into your lap. As long as you keep progressing forward when it comes to your skills, sharing your accomplishments with your industry, and giving as many good vibes back as you receive, you'll be on your way. To do something you've never done, you must be someone you never been. You don't have to be great to get started, but you have to get started to be great. You must be fearless and stop letting others control your life. God did not give you a spirit of fear. There are no limits in life on what you can do. So, find the inner you and walk with wisdom toward your future, making the best use of your time.

Head Shepherd
P.O.G
Loving Ministry

Mind
OPTIMISM

H ope and confidence about the future. Looking at the positive aspects of things. It is also a hopeful anticipation that future events will be favorable. Basically, it is seeing and expecting the best in all things. Change how you look at your life. See the glass being half full and not half empty. God has so much in store for your life. When you have a heart filled with love and a peace of mind, you have a more positive attitude. Don't let the negative things in life bring you down. Live in the now and be happy with who you are. Do you tend to see the positive even in trying situations? Or do you assume the worst and focus on the negative? When it comes to how we view the world, most of us fall into one of two categories: optimists or pessimists. Whatever category you fall into has a lot to do with who you are. Sometimes it's hard to be happy when you think about negative things that are happening in the world. It's harder still when the people around you constantly complain about all those things that are happening. But you do not have to join ranks with the pessimists. In fact, it's extra important to be optimistic when there's negativity surrounding you. People who are optimistic tend to experience less stress and feel a greater appreciation for other people. In short, just be happy!

Head Shepherd
P.O.G.
Loving Ministry

Mind
PAY ATTENTION

Deuteronomy 7:12 NIV, "If you pay attention to these laws and are careful to follow them, then the LORD your God will keep his covenant of love with you, as he swore to your ancestors."

In society today, people have become so selfish and arrogant. You may have known someone all your life, yet you never really understood them. You never listened to or believed in what they were telling you. Now you feel you don't really know them at all because you never took the time to consider their emotions. Why is it that you can know someone your whole life, but you don't know who they really are? Because you were only concerned about yourself. We live our lives always consumed with ourselves. Never giving others opinion any thought. When will we learn we must coexist in the world? If we want true peace, we must learn to share different ideas so we can all get along. Stop selling others short and listen to what they say. It may make a difference in your day. When we are able to share different thoughts with one another, then we'll be able to understand each other. There is always more than one side to every story. As people, we must stop thinking we know it all, and share an ear to listen. For humanity to move forward as a species, we must take a look at our inner selves. What emotion drives us: envy, jealousy, or arrogance? We must learn how to change these negative feelings and turn them into something positive, like love, joy, and happiness. Then, we will be able to change the frequency of the universe, and start living like God wants us to live. Take time to listen when someone is talking. You may learn something.

Head Shepherd
P.O.G.
Loving Ministry

Mind
PERSUASION

Is the action or effect of persuading someone or of being persuaded to do or believe something. A belief or a set of beliefs, especially religious or political ones. There are so many people who think they know what is best for you in life. They have so many ideas and opinions on how you should live your life. Why is it we are so quick to believe men and not God? Our heavenly Father knows human hearts, so if you listen to them, you should be on guard. There are many people trying to persuade you to believe in things that you should not do. Trust in God because he will never mislead you. The world has changed so dramatically I know it's hard to know who is trying to trick you. Do not be deceived. God cannot be mocked. A man reaps what he sows. "The one who sows to please his sinful nature from that nature will reap destruction, but the one who sows to please the spirit from the spirit will reap eternal life." When you are able to move people with God's words, then you're making a difference in their lives. The world needs more people who love humanity. Wake up every morning and think to yourself, *How can I make a difference in someone's life?* Words are just words. Kindness and love are action. Help others and embrace God. We are often hurt by others, not realizing what we do is what matters. When you live and walk in God's words, then people will start taking you seriously.

Head Shepherd
P.O.G.
Loving Ministry

Mind
PLAN

Do you know what you want to do with your life? Many of us go through life never knowing our true potential. We all have a special talent that we do better than others. Humans are almost incapable of being 100% satisfied with their current situation, no matter how balanced and successful others consider it to be. This is because we tend to get to specific spots in life without any meaning, aim, or direction. To avoid this haphazard lifestyle, you need to learn how to make a life plan. There is also a high chance that most people consider their wishes and dreams unrealistic or unachievable. There comes a time in everyone's life when you must have faith in the impossible. When you're able to believe in yourself and the heavenly Father, all things become possible. Just remember when you fail to plan, you plan to fail. When you are at your darkest hour, that is when the Holy Spirit Steps in. Success isn't always about greatness; it's about consistency. Consistent hard work gains success. Greatness will come. When something is important enough for you, you do it even if the odds are against you. Once you forget what you're worth, you forget what you deserve. The secret to change is to focus all of your energy not on fighting the old, but building the new.

Head Shepherd
P.O.G.
Loving Ministry

Mind POSSIBLE

....

What does Jesus mean by "possible"? Does he mean that we will be able to walk on water? Escape trials and tribulations? Overcome illness of any kind? Even avoid death? Throughout the history of the church Gods, people have meant live as it is. Water is water, and in many ways, we are subject to its continuing power. Those called to the gospel has been more apt to enter trials and tribulations then to escape it. And death comes to all people, no matter how faithful. So what is it that will not be "impossible"? It may be this: It is not impossible for those who have been marked with the cross of Christ to walk toward the power of destruction with the conviction that God's will for life to flourish nonetheless prevails. It is not impossible to fight darkness with light, hatred with love, illness with hope. It is not impossible for us to stand at the graveside of our loved ones and sing of a day when every tear will be wiped away from every eye. What's not impossible? That God's kingdom endures even through us.

Head Shepherd
P.O.G.
Loving Ministry

Mind
PROMISES

Many of us live with unfulfilled dreams and goals. We make plans that never materialize, and there are destinations we never reach. Moses was Gods servant. He reluctantly accepted the call to lead the Hebrew people out of slavery in Egypt to the Promised Land. With God's help, Moses secured their release from Farrow and led this rebellion and the complaining people across the desert. For forty years, Moses endured their grumbling. On the way, Moses received the 10 commandments from God, and taught these words to the people. Later, however, Moses failed to obey one of God's orders, and as a result, the Lord would not allow him to enter the Promised Land. God let Moses view the Land and promised that the people would enter it. Moses died with that promise in his heart. We are not always allowed to see the results of our labor as God's children. We cannot see the kingdom of Heaven. Instead, we trust Jesus's promise that we will dwell with him there. We eagerly wait, longing to receive the inheritance God has prepared for us.

Head Shepherd
P.O.G
Loving Ministry

Mind
PURPOSE

....

Why are we here on this planet? What is our purpose in life? We live life day in, and day out, not knowing the real reason for our existence. We have been seeking answers from authority figures and clergyman to tell us what we should be doing in life. Why have we not called on the Almighty Father? He is the beginning and the end to all the problems in life. He has given you the answer to why you are here on this Earth. We only have to read the book to understand who we really are in life. Stop believing in men with all his division. Thoughts are your frequencies that connect to your higher source which is God. There is a creator for all things in the world. Why can't you believe someone created you into existence? Stop feeling lost and confused about which direction to go in life. The moment you stay positive is when God is guiding you through life. God has given you a mind to create whatever reality you want. Think of yourself being a happy person, content with life. Remind yourself every day that you are a child of God. Then, you will be able to manifest the world you want to live in. Take time to silence your mind. Listen to the universe tell you why you are here on this Earth. We need to be in tune with one another in order to change how the world works. The true reason we are here is to make a difference in someone's life. Just be happy with who you are. Love yourself and everyone around you, regardless of who they are. That is your why.

Head Shepherd
P.O.G.
Loving Ministry

Mind
REJUVENATE

Give new energy or vigor to revitalize. Job 33:25 NIV, "Let their flesh be renewed like a child's; let them be restored as in the days of their youth."

There comes a time in life when your old ways don't work anymore. It's time to start anew. Think of ways you can become creative with your life. Stop letting people tell you that you can't do something. If you want to be happier and healthier and are ready to make a lifestyle change, there are several ways to do that. Self-care is an important thing that is often overlooked in modern society. Rejuvenation for life is important for everyone in today's hectic world. It seems everywhere you turn there are people who are stressed out, burned out, and exhausted. A good choice is to calm down and set aside some time for yourself so you can clear your mind, refocus, and approach issues from a new angle. Life is about creating and living experiences that are worth sharing. People who are fun, loving, and energetic tend to live a healthier lifestyle. When your feelings about yourself are improved, you have the ability to cope with stress and enjoy life more. If you feel you could be more fun, loving, and energetic, you can do this by changing your outlook on love. Just love yourself and God!

Head Shepherd
P.O.G.
Loving Ministry

Mind
RESPONSIBILITY

An opportunity is your best opening to add value, to people and ways that best align with who you are and most energize your spirit. Opportunities are found in your greatest opening, to give not your greatest chance to get. We as spiritual beings must be ready for whatever God has coming our way. When the time comes, you must be ready to accept the responsibility. But the one who does not know and does things deserving punishment will be beaten with few blows. Much will be demanded from everyone who has been given, and much more will be asked from the one who has been entrusted with much. The reason the humans are here on this Earth is to be of service to one another. When you live your life doing for others you will always be ready for whatever comes your way. It is said that you only have fifteen minutes of fame. When it comes, will you be ready to take advantage of it? You can't get from here to there until you know where your destination is. Talent is nothing without dedication and discipline, and dedication and discipline are talents in themselves. Life has a keen sense of humor, and it is all the more enjoyable when we are laughing with it. We have a choice on how we want to live our life. We can either choose to trek through life as though it is a burden full of drudgery and monotony, or we can realize that life is as grand as we believe it to be.

Head Shepherd
P.O.G.
Loving Ministry

Mind
SANITY OR INSANITY

As I walk around in society today, its seems like we are out of an episode of *The Twilight Zone*. Everyone is wearing a mask with the look of doom in their eyes. Why have we given this enemy so much control over our lives? Elders, you must think about your children and the future of their families. When will you say, "No more. I'm tired of letting you tell me what to do!"? Stop listening to those lies of the media and letting them program your mind. Take off your mask and speak out, letting them know this is not right. This enemy has destroyed countless lives in so many countries by poisoning us. Why can't we all see what's really going on? They are taking control over our lives by telling us who lives or dies. It's time to wake up and fight for what is right. This devil will never stop until you tell him, "No more. My God is in control." Not just one person; we all must stand up together and fight. We can't be divided anymore. It's time to come together and reunite for one cause: to defeat this wicked enemy! Your words have power when you speak out against injustice. This enemy is only a few; we are millions when we stand together in God's words. This war has already been won. Why do we keep repeating the past? Start living right. When you don't learn from the past, you are doomed to repeat it. God has put us here to live in peace with each other. Show love and kindness towards one another.

Head Shepherd
P.O.G.
Loving Ministry

Mind SHOW

There is a saying: "When people show you who they are, believe them." It is often applied to people who reveal themselves time and time again to have poor judgment and behavior. Those around them do not want to accept that this is their true character. They make all sorts of excuses for the bad behavior. Jesus time and again revealed himself to have perfect character and be divine as well as human. Over and over, he worked miracles by healing the sick and taming treacherous weather. Even after all that, his disciples continue to ask themselves, *what sort of man is this?* Even though Jesus showed them clearly and consistently who he was, they still had questions about his identity and nature. We too can have questions about Jesus sometimes, but the more we learn about his amazing life, death, and resurrection, the more his power and his goodness are revealed to us. Jesus has indeed showed us who he is, so, as the saying goes, we should believe him.

Head Shepherd
P.O.G.
Loving Ministry

Mind
THE STATE OF THE WORLD

Life is like a formula: you have a theory, observation, and conclusion. There is so much going on in this world that it is overwhelming. 2020 was the year of revelation. We lost loved ones due to the pandemic and due to gun violence at the hands of police or our own. We had the election in November. I have never seen an administration that is so disrespectful to the American people. However, I strongly urge you to pay attention to what's really going on. All the information from experts who tell you one thing one minute, and then they change it to something else the next minute. All these different theories about the state of the world. Something sounds so far-fetched, but when you keep hearing the same thing over and over again, you can't help but wonder, *is it true?* One thing my grandmother always said is that everybody can't tell the same lie. That phrase resonated with me. It made me listen with discernment; it made me pay more attention. This world is in turmoil, and right now, the only thing we can do is pray. Keep your eyes open and look at the fine print. Be still and listen. Don't be so fast to respond. Let it resonate first, and do research. Then pray as if Jesus was coming back tomorrow. The Bible tells us the state of the world will grow darker as we near the end of the age. So, my POG family, I urge you to please pray and stay woke.

Lady Shepherd
P.O.G.
Loving Ministry

Mind
STAY POSITIVE

....

A few days ago, I started receiving telephone calls from my siblings. I was driving at the time, then the one last call came in. It was my mom. And I knew it was something urgent. When I was able to pull over, I listened to the message. My mom said my sister was found not breathing and unconscious in her home, and she was rushed to the emergency room. At that point, I immediately began to pray, and asked the Father to be with her and comfort me. My other sister got on social media and asked for everyone to pray for my sister. And everyone did as she asked. When I got home, I called my mom and told her we need to go see my sister and pray for her. I was regretting the trip because I did not want to see her in that state, because she is always filled with life. We went on the journey to the hospital, and my heart sank when I saw her in that state. We immediately begin to pray around her bed. Then, other family members and friends showed up and did the same. I was feeling lonely and sad, and I wanted to leave so I would not have to see her in that state. But something in my mind kept telling me to hold on, that change was coming. When the last family member showed up, God stepped in and woke her up. She knew who we were and had a smile on her face. So, I'm telling you there is power in prayer. Don't be too quick to believe God is not a miracle worker. There is power in each and every one of us. When we unite in God's words, there is nothing we cannot do.

Head Shepherd
P.O.G.
Loving Ministry

Mind
STOP HATING

"Love your enemies as you love yourself" doesn't mean you have to accept what they are doing to you. Hating is a low vibration energy. It drains you of your power. Have you ever heard the saying, "no bond is stronger than two people who hate the same person? It turns out there is actually some truth to that statement despite hating people being a socially unacceptable act except on a few occasions when people have the guts and strong emotions to motivate. Two people sharing their negative opinions about a person often pays off in a form of a new or stronger connection. If you are a generally positive, forgiving person the concept of hating others, much less someone you barely know, is likely a foreign concept to you. Try the loving kindness practice as a reminder to connect with the energy of an open heart, a practice that has no intention of leading anywhere other than the wish for oneself and others to be happy and well. The deepest expression of that wish would be for one's own heart to be filled with the wisdom that leads to no longer acting in a way that causes pain to oneself or others, which is compassion. To stop hating, you have to go within your soul and stop seeing the world like man has told you to. Understand who you are and your creation of something remarkable. We are all living as one in this universe. It's time to start loving, caring for, and sharing with someone.

Head Shepherd
P.O.G.
Loving Ministry

Mind STRUCTURE

To have a new life, you must tear down the old one and rebuild a new one. Whenever you're building anything, you need to have structure. You need to know how your life will be in order to rebuild it. You need to have some kind of plan, or blueprint, before you start to put your life together again. Before you take a trip to a destination, there is a map to show you the directions to get there. We need structure in our lives to hold them together. You are an architect for your life. You can design any future for your life. Your mind is the perfect weapon: It can build or destroy your future. It is up to you to make the right decisions. Construct something beyond your imagination. Look up to Christ and let him help you build a solid foundation for your life. You have something inside of you; it is time to let the world see it. Be that master builder and create a world of possibilities. Take every step you need to. Fall a few times and build on that. The hammer is in your hand, so start building who God created you to be. It is not going to be easy. You are going to feel some pain, but that comes from building. The hard work you put in today will be worth it tomorrow. You must master the skills to achieve great heights. Put in the work even when you don't feel like it. That is when you can accomplish anything. Build strength and pride. Encourage yourself to be a better human being. Build that person that you want to be for someone who believes in Christ.

Head Shepherd
P.O.G.
Loving Ministry

Mind
STRUGGLING

You do not rise to the level of your goals; you fall to the level of your systems. As spiritual beings, why do we struggle? We struggle in our finances, health, and relationships. When will we start living the words of God? We have let this enemy fill this earth with darkness. 1 Corinthians 10:13 NIV, "No temptation has overtaken you except what is common to mankind. And God is faithful; he will not let you be tempted beyond what you can bear. But when you are tempted, he will also provide a way out so that you can endure it." No matter how great your life may be, you will eventually deal with disappointment, setbacks, failures, and even loss and trauma. Everyone must face difficult situations, and everyone must come up with effective ways to deal with and come back from these situations. Sometimes we need to cope with things that happen to us, and other times we must cope with things that happened within us. Some events may require us to deal with both internal and external demands. Having a clear idea of what you want and where you want to be can inspire you to push through. If you have no clear goal of what you want, you won't be as motivated to overcome adversity. You won't keep yourself as diligent and energized as you need to be to succeed. Define what you want to achieve, and it will help you be more persistent in finding a way to overcome your burdens.

Head Shepherd
P.O.G.
Loving Ministry

Mind
SUPPORTING

God says, "Do unto others as you would have them do unto you." As a society, we have become so conditioned to only think about ourselves. Even in some churches, when a visitor comes, we do not try to meet or greet them. Instead, we talk about them for taking our parking space or our seat in church. In some families, when a sibling is trying to do better for himself, we do not encourage or help them out, only thinking of ourselves. It's time, P.O.G., for us to start supporting other members of our P.O.G. family. We can do this by going to their businesses, sharing your ideas with them, and just being nice in general. God wants us to be a nation of one by loving, sharing, and caring for one another. You cannot win a war if you are just standing by yourself. When you have unity amongst the people, the power in each and every one of us will become as one. There is power in a name of Jesus. Let's start supporting and helping each other again. Stop tearing down and start building up so that we may be the winners in the end.

Head Shepherd
P.O.G.
Loving Ministry

Mind
TEACHERS

Society is full of spiritual teachers and cultures who encourage us to do what we want. They teach us to visualize the things we want to manifest them. The underlining philosophy seems to prevail: Do what makes you happy, and do not consider how it affects others. This teaching appeals to many people because it gives individuals a sense of control over their lives. It teaches us to focus on ourselves and not others. This, however, is not the truth that Jesus teaches. Jesus urges us to put God first and do God's will. He teaches us to love others and to care for others as he did. Jesus's ways are not easy and seem to be becoming less popular. There are other spiritual teachings but if we are P.O.G., God's will is the truth; it is the way. When we follow Jesus by doing God's will and loving others, our focus turns upward and outward. It is the way to create a world of peace and true joy.

Head Shepherd
P.O.G.
Loving Ministry

Mind
TEAM

....

If you do what's easy, your life will be hard. But if you do what's hard, your life will be easy. Instead of worrying about what you cannot control, shift your energy to what you can create. We all need a team of people in our life to help us move through the obstacles of life. Someone to pick us up when we trip and fall. When you surround yourself with love, there's nothing you cannot do, because the positive energy is with you. You need someone to talk to, to help you understand the problems you go through. When a group of people's minds are on the same page, they can bring this idea to life. Visualize you and your team making the plays to achieve victory. A successful team starts with the right people – those who value working toward a common goal – and goals originated from and respectful to everyone's ideas. To build trust in the team, first you must model teams for your own team. Have confidence to work together as a team by relying on the simple idea that they are trusted. Teamwork makes the dream work! Point out when you have good people around you who are willing to be loving, caring, and sharing with one another. Then, we are doing God's will. In that moment, we will be able to create whatever reality we desire. Be a servant of the people and help them build a more positive world. Once you stop talking and start taking action daily, that's when your life truly changes for the better. Take action; don't make excuses. Winners do whatever it takes. Enjoy the journey with friends and you will win in the end.

Head Shepherd
P.O.G.
Loving Ministry

Mind

TEAMWORK

There is no "I" in teamwork; we all need someone in our life to make the dream work. When we can overcome our selfish ways, and let other people help when they need to, we are realizing the creative side of us. Be mindful of everyone that you let on your team because everyone around you isn't always there for you. It's not about the amount of people around you but the quality of people. Keep the Bad News Bears people off your team. When someone genuinely wants to be on your team, they will not expect something back from you. With the right people on your team, it will become a dream team! We are all the same we just want someone to appreciate us for who we are. Like attracts like, so be around positive people. Never let another person's opinion determine who you are. When you're connected with the universal God, he will always send the right people your way. Think about the people you want in your life. You manifest the things you concentrate on. Whenever people can come together and work things out, it is when God is there with us. Then all of life's problems won't seem so bad. It is the connection that keeps us together and close to God. It's time to stop hating each other. When we can know who we really are, then we will be able to create and manifest whatever reality we want here on this Earth.

Head Shepherd
P.O.G.
Loving Ministry

Mind
THE LAW

In today's society, laws are structured to work out for the better of thee, and not for the least of thee. In a P.O.G. video, we were speaking about the laws of the land. It has come to my attention that there is a law on the books called affluenza, meaning that someone of wealth can't determine right from wrong. Their symptoms are lack of motivation, feelings of guilt, and a sense of isolation. It's vital that you are aware of these laws. I have some examples. A very wealthy family living in the suburbs in a gated community with parents who have good jobs found out that their daughter was selling heroin. This young lady started selling heroin to a minor, and the kid ended up dying. Another example is that a young man living with his parents in a very wealthy neighborhood was accused of date rape. They both got off because of the law affluenza. Now let's stop and think for a minute. If this was an average situation, and a person was not wealthy, the laws will not accommodate him or her because of their financial status. The laws are not up to par with the powers that be. It is vital that we as P.O.G. know about our government, because one voice or vote will not be heard, but with many we can try to make a difference. Man's laws are only temporary, because, at any time, he can change them to fit his needs. But God's laws are eternal.

Head Shepherd
P.O.G.
Loving Ministry

Mind
THE POWER OF LOVE

Colleges can impart knowledge and confer degrees, but they cannot force their graduates to use this knowledge for the benefits of others. Knowledge is like a seed planted in the garden of the mind that bears fruit, some to satisfy our curiosity and some to share with others.

Teachers have no assurance that students will not use this knowledge for selfish ends that seem a misuse of education. Another element needs to be added to knowledge: love. The love Paul speaks of here cannot be mandated. It is God's gift. It must be experienced, and it reaches full bloom when we place others first. God's love is the greatest force on Earth for good. Jesus said, "God so loved the world, that He gave His only begotten Son, that whoever believes in Him shall not perish, but have eternal life." Jesus also taught, "No one has greater love than this, to lay down one's life for one's friends." The love that "builds up our lives is eternal. It is the priceless gift God gives us in Christ Jesus."

Head Shepherd
P.O.G.
Loving Ministry

Mind THINK

The enemy has placed a contract on our young men. It seems that every time we turn on the news, we hear of young men getting killed. Even in the James Vandyke case, it took a judge and a jury to find out this man was guilty after a crime of overkill. The enemy is so crafty he wants to wage a war with people of power and people with no power. He wants to confuse society so there will be chaos here on earth. When this craziness begins, the government will step in place and call it Marshall law. And once this happens, all the power will be turned over to them and your freedom will be gone. It's time to put God back in your schools, back in your homes, and back into your relationships. Only then we will have the chance to stop this from happening. God says when you pray in unity, he will always listen; so, let's start praying.

Head Shepherd
P.O.G.
Loving Ministry

Mind
THOUGHTS!

Isaiah 55:8 NIV, "'For my thoughts are not your thoughts, neither are your ways my ways', declares the LORD.'"

Your mind is a creative, smart part of your body. It has the capability to determine the outcome of your life. Have you ever heard of what a person thinks they are in life? Your thoughts are frequencies that connect you to the universal God. When you are able to have a pure heart, your Father will grant you pure thoughts. It is crucial that you keep guard over what you let in your mind. Try to reprogram yourself to have thoughts of greatness and healing in your life. Don't let others' opinions turn you from these thoughts. You must believe so you can receive the goodness in life. Before going to sleep at night, tell yourself, "I am powerful. I am grateful," and right away when you wake up do the same. These are some examples but you can use any positive words that will help you become better. Always keep control over your emotions; try to be happy at all times. When you have thoughts of positive energy flowing through your body it can heal you. Stay away from negative thoughts and people. Surround yourself with positive people who want the best for you. Take time to enjoy all the beautiful places in the world like a tropical paradise. Have good things to say about everyone you meet. Love them as you love yourself. Just be happy about and content with your wonderful life. Life is too short to worry about things out of your control. When you can navigate through the storms of life, you will have authority over your life. You will feel like a bird being set free. Now you will be able to choose your destiny in life. You have the power over your thoughts. Just keep them positive, and you will be all right. Happiness brings success.

Head Shepherd
P.O.G.
Loving Ministry

Mind
TITLES

....

Why are people always wanting to be better than others in life? We spend years in school studying to be different than others. We have put titles on one another to know who is better. God created all of us to be human and love each other. Having a degree doesn't make you someone of greater importance than everyone else. Just because you have an office and a parking space doesn't mean you're better than others. Know you are a human just like everyone else. If you are a good person, you don't need a title to define who you are in life. A title is a tool used by the enemy to keep us divided from each other. If we leave our hearts open to the possibility of human connection and don't raise barriers out of fear of our differences, then we can literally change the world. There are times in your life when you must put away your title and open your heart! Why do we need a title to validate who we are in life? Be a person with empathy for humanity. All the riches in the world will never show you love. Trust in your abilities to achieve things in life with love. Titles are a tool of the enemy to keep us from our greatness. When we are divided, we are not able to connect to Christ's energy and be as one. When we are able to be as one and connect to the body of Christ, there is no force in the universe that could stop us from having the reality we choose. It's time to start loving, caring, and sharing with one another again. We are all-powerful when we stand as one in God's eye. The power of your name is better than an impressive title.

Head Shepherd
P.O.G.
Loving Ministry

Mind
TOMORROW

Tomorrow: a mystical land where 98 percent of all human productivity, motivation, and achievement is stored. Do you know how you think? It can be just about any task. There are no particular characteristics of the task except that you don't feel like doing it, at least not right now. The thing is you shouldn't think that way. The time comes for action and to do as you say. The reason we waste time is that we don't have clear goals and desires that we're working towards. When you determine what you really want from your day, year, or life, it gives you focus and direction. At the beginning of each week, write out what you want to accomplish. This can be as simple as making a to-do list with specific tasks. When you find yourself wasting time, go back to your list of goals and focus on doing the next task. The decisions you make in your everyday life will determine your destiny. We must all suffer one of two things: the pain of deciding or the pain of regret, or disappointment. The truth is that God has been answering you all your life, but you cannot receive the answers until you listen. Matthews 6:34 NIV, "Therefore do not worry about tomorrow, for tomorrow will worry about itself. Each day has enough trouble of its own."

Head Shepherd
P.O.G.
Loving Ministry

Mind
TRANSITION

The process or period of changing from one state or condition to another. God is with us in every season of our life. When we face the unknown, we can trust that He is in control and working out every situation for our good. Life is so unpredictable; at any moment, it can throw you a curve ball. For a long time, you have been doing things a certain way. All of a sudden, you have to make a change. Now, you have to be taught to do things in a different way than you're used to doing them. Your mind is filled with negative emotions, trying to make you quit. Don't give up, and keep the faith. God will get you through this. Just believe in yourself and your skills to be able to adapt to any situation. God has not brought you this far to just give up on you. You are a creator; you can build a new life in any environment. Know what you love and seek out those things to fill the void. Change is all around us. No matter how hard we try, we will never be able to keep up with all the latest developments. The fact that change and innovation are accelerating rapidly makes it even more difficult to stay on top of the game. No matter how difficult it is to keep learning and to keep adapting, it is crucial for your success in life. If you don't like something, change it. If you can't change it, change your attitude.

Head Shepherd
P.O.G.
Loving Ministry

Mind TROUBLE

In many movies, there is a scene where a character is in trouble, and suddenly, he or she sees someone who looks like a friend. The character in trouble hesitates to believe that they might be rescued from danger at first. But, as the story continues, the character learns to trust that this is indeed a good person who is there to help. The disciples out in their boat being battered by the rough sea suddenly saw someone who looked like Jesus walking on the water towards them. This was so hard to believe! Was it a ghost? They were afraid to hope it was their Lord. But it was the Lord, the ultimate good guy, who had come to save them. He urged them to take part and have courage. He would never abandon them. And so, the Lord Jesus walked across the waves toward his beloved friends. In our times of trouble, on the rocky sea of life, Jesus walks to us as well, to be with us and to save us from the storms.

Head Shepherd
P.O.G.
Loving Ministry

Mind
TRUST YOURSELF

If you find from your own experience that something is a fact, and it contradicts what someone with authority has written down, then you must abandon the authority and base your reasoning on your own finding. The world is so out of order we don't know what to believe. People are walking around afraid of being next to one another. The enemy has made humanity so confused. You were created with a belief system that will give you clarity. We must stop waiting on someone to save us. Just be your own savior. Tap into your real power and believe there are higher forces than men. When we are able to think for ourselves, the enemy has no control over our lives. The universe works in mysterious ways. Just know God is in control. Don't let people be telling you to do this or that in your life. You already know how you feel about things in your life. It isn't our responsibility to change minds, but it is our responsibility to at least give people the option of knowing the truth. Stay positive and trust that everything will be OK. Your thoughts are your perception of life, so have beautiful ones. Life is not easy and there will be many situations that come your way that can cause you stress and anxiety. But no matter what your situation is right now, you have to trust yourself and stay calm and positive. We have to learn to trust that little voice inside of your head. When you sense that something is wrong, believe in your intuition and trust God. You will never go wrong.

Head Shepherd
P.O.G.
Loving Ministry

Mind
UNDERSTAND

When things go wrong in our lives, as they sometimes do for all of us, we can feel very much alone. During those dark nights, the question arises: Is there anyone who suffers with me, who can comfort me? In those sad and lonely moments, we long for a loving companion in our struggles, someone who understands what we are experiencing and can help us get through even the worst of times. The prophet Isaiah told the people of Jerusalem some very good news: The Lord would not ignore them or desert them. Instead, the Lord would plead their cause, share their sadness, and dry their tears. The Lord still does this for us. Even when we have brought the trouble on ourselves, we can never lose our place in God's heart, and we are never far from God's embrace. God is the answer to our loneliness and our sorrow. Knowing that, we can face the future with courage and confidence.

Head Shepherd
P.O.G.
Loving Ministry

Mind
UPSETTING

It's that time again when everyone's rushing and trying to make their season bright and make sure everything is perfect. God says there is no perfect person, so how can there be a perfect thing? We all have sinned before God. So, stop worrying about what others do, and worry about yourself. People say things, and they don't realize how harsh they sound. Have you ever encountered someone who says something, and they have no idea that they insulted you? But at the end of the day, you feel some type of way? You don't want rock the boat because you don't want to start an argument. So, you hold in your feelings and how upset you are, which is not the best thing to do. We should learn to communicate with one another and not hesitate to say what's in our mind or heart. Remember, a gentle answer turns away wrath, but a harsh word stirs up anger. Have faith; once bad feelings have their way with you, feeling better is not far behind. Don't worry that painful emotions might hang around forever. They won't. The only pain that can potentially last forever is a painful struggle not to feel real emotions again. That you can do for the rest of your life. But who wants to?

Head Shepherd
P.O.G.
Loving Ministry

Mind
VISION

A while ago, the enemy showed us his vision of how he wants the world to be. Many bought into it and started to worry about and fear the situation. Whenever someone can control your perception, they can control your world. The enemy knows your thoughts are where your power is, so whatever you think is going to be your reality. If we want to change the world, we must first change the way we see it. We are all connected. We must be on the same accord to make this happen. Your thoughts are frequencies that connect you to God. That is why it is so important to pray in unity. When we all come together and stand as one, God truly hears us. No one will ever do it for you. Nobody can do it for you. And do not doubt yourself, because there are plenty of people who will do that for you. Stay dedicated to your vision. Believe that you can make a difference in this world. Reject every negative thought that the enemy sent your way. Be consistent and self-disciplined and exhibit self-control so you can develop great character. Whatever may happen, never yield to obstacles but advance more strongly with wisdom, encouraged to meet them as our heart let us. Life is but test after test. Be prepared to be tested with fear, failure, and loss of health and wealth. Just keep your vision of changing things to something of greatness.

Head Shepherd
P.O.G.
Loving Ministry

Mind
WAIT

....

How often do we wait each day? We wait at traffic lights. We wait in line at the store, or the bank, or the drive through. We wait for our meals to be cooked, and for a loved one to come and see us. Waiting is an unavoidable part of life. The promise requires us to wait for God, too. We wait for God's instruction, mercy, and interventions as we face the challenges of our lives. There is a word in Hebrew that can translate either as wait or hope. When you think about it, when we wait, we hope. We hope for God's action. The people like us do not want to be disappointed by waiting. So how do we wait? What do we do when you have hope in the Lord? We learn, and God is willing to teach. We act humbly and follow the example of Christ. We leave our sins and failures in God's hands, trusting in God's forgiveness and restoration to purposeful living. After all, this has been God's nature and intention from the beginning. Hope empowers and directs our waiting. Hoping in the Lord is never in vain.

Head Shepherd
P.O.G.
Loving Ministry

Mind

WHERE IS YOUR PRIDE?

Many of us have an instinctual allergy to pridefulness and boasting. We do not want to be gloating; we downplay our talents; we refuse to toot our own horn. To be sure, there are some who take things entirely to the opposite direction. There are some who have no problem with boasting or tooting their own horn. And many of us who are so committed to not being like them refuse to boast or take pride in ourselves at all. Boastfulness and pride are not bad things in and of themselves. It's a matter of where one places one's pride, and what one chooses to boast about. Paul tells us that if we are going to boast, we should boast in the Lord. So, there is truly no problem in boasting about a particular gift you might have, perhaps for singing. Paul's point is this: we boast and are proud of singing of gifts that God gave. In fact, to do otherwise might be to deny the gift that God has provided. God has given us many gifts. We can be thankful for them, boast of them, and use them to enlarge God's kingdom.

Head Shepherd
P.O.G.
Loving Ministry

Mind
WHY (1)

Good morning, people of God. So, the other day I was watching this disturbing documentary called *Surviving R Kelly*. I was really confused by the whole situation. How was he able to hang out at the high school to recruit underage girls? For the parents: Why did you allow your daughters to go with a person with a questionable reputation to be around your child? To his ex-wife: Why was he able to degrade your soul, but the next day you're on social media giving him praise? Why do we compartmentalize bad behavior? He is a genius when it comes to his music, but as a person he is a monster. You have to ask yourself, is money the root of our existence? A lot of people commented that if these were white girls this would not have gone so far. But it makes me ask the question is it really about that? These girls all had something in common: They were all poor, naive, and they all had this scarlet letter, meaning that at some point in their lives, they were molested or suffered from some type of abuse. I just find it interesting how someone with a limited education can pick up on that. He was a hunter searching for his prey. That is how the enemy operates — he catches you at your weakest moment. He gets you to trust him, and then asks you to do things that are wrong and immoral. So, I ask my young sistahs and brothers to please stand up and say something when you see someone who is suffering. We will keep praying for all who is involved.

Lady Shepherd
P.O.G.
Loving Ministry

Mind
WISDOM

Everything has a beginning, a source. Wisdom comes from something greater than itself. We cannot order it from Amazon or purchase it from a stock market. We need to find a source of wisdom before we can understand it. We experience the wisdom of God all around us in the dependability and orderliness of creation. It is seen in the adaptability in the animal kingdom. It is seen in the decisions of kind, honest people. Awe of the creator is the beginning of wisdom. I don't think the opposite of wisdom is ignorance, but rather arrogance, which exalts itself to the exclusion of everyone and everything else. Self-centered action failed to acknowledge the need for others. Wisdom lies in the thinking about future consequences of our actions and how they will affect others. Wisdom is rooted in God, and we pray for spirit to help us bare the fruit of this wisdom at work in our lives. Wisdom is a gift, rather any accomplishments. It is the opening of ourselves to the gift and abilities in others and in all creations.

Head Shepherd
P.O.G.
Loving Ministry

Mind

WORK ETHIC

Learn to work smart, not hard; then, your life will be easier. You are taught at birth about work. You must instill into your child in the beginning lessons about work ethic as they see their parents go off to work. Some people want it to happen; some wish it would happen; others make it happen. If you don't build your dream, someone else will hire you to help build theirs. You can't rely just on motivation to do stuff. It's better to form habits, be disciplined, and have a system in place so that you get things done even when you're not motivated. You must be willing to do the things today others won't do in order for you to have the thing tomorrow that the others won't have. It is all about the mindset. You have to remember that everything moves in frequency, and if you want something you have to imagine that you are already doing it. The universe will open the door for you and will lead you to your biggest goals in life. Regardless of what you are trying to aim for in life, know and attract it into existence, and you shall have it. But never forget to always pray as well, because we need the help of God to help us get there. Focus, work hard, and watch the results. Work ethic is one of the most valuable attributes employers look for in their prospective employees in every industry. Employers prefer employees with excellent work ethics because they are reliable, disciplined, and dedicated. Showing that you have the value associated with a good work ethic can increase your employment ability, and help you position yourself for better job opportunities. Colossions 3:23-24 NIV, "Whatever you do, work at it with all your heart, as working for the Lord, not for human masters, since you know that you will receive an inheritance from the Lord as a reward. It is the Lord Christ you are serving."

Head Shepherd
P.O.G.
Loving Ministry

Mind

WORLD GONE MAD

From the beginning of time, we asked God to let man rule over us. We needed someone to tell us how to live our lives. God said he would do this only if man kept His principles and Commandments. He agreed to this, and it started out going well. Then, the devil didn't like how well the people were living. He decided that he would corrupt man. He tempted him with greed and arrogance, making him believe he was a God over his subjects. When some are given power, they can become a tyrant, abusing their authority they have over us. There were even some who rewrote the Bible to fit their agenda. They told us lies about history and who we really were in life. They did not want you to know that no man has authority over us but your heavenly Father. Man began to take God out of everything – school, the workplace, and home. He made us selfish people, only concerned about ourselves and not others. He knew where the real power was, and that is unity, when we are together. That is why men love division like color, religion, and politics to keep us divided. He has studied every aspect of our lives so he can keep his control. These rulers are not human, but wicked entities. They will use all types of technology to control how we think. The time has come for us to take back our thoughts and start believing in the Almighty One. Together, we are the body of Christ which can defeat the evil one. We are pure energy when we stand as one. We must have the same thoughts to manifest a better reality. We have to let love guide us if we want this world to be heaven on Earth. We all were given free will to choose to do for others and stop only thinking about ourselves. It doesn't take much to make someone's day, just a smile. Have you noticed when you smile the whole world smiles back? Be that person who makes a difference in someone's life. Let others know that they are a recipient of God's love.

Head Shepherd
P.O.G.
Loving Ministry

Mind
WORRY

....

S uccess is peace of mind which is a direct result of self-satisfaction in knowing you made the effort to become the best of which you are capable. Stop letting the enemy fill your mind with worry. The universal God has not given you any reason to worry. God is in control of your life; just let him in. Worry does not empty tomorrow of its sorrows; it empties today of its strength. It starts with a negative thought that creates another few fearful thoughts. Before you know it, there is a storm brewing in your mind, making you think irrationally and draining your mental and physical energy. Take a deep breath. Hold it for a moment and then exhale. Feel more relaxed? Breathing exercises are one way to help you when you worry. You must learn different ways to relax your mind and body. Being relaxed can help ease stress. It can also relieve anxiety, depression, and sleep problems. We all worry and get upset from time to time. It's a normal part of life, right? But when that anxiety or anger takes over and you can't calm down, being able to calm yourself in the moment is often easier said than done. Allow yourself to say that you're anxious or angry. When you face your feeling and allow yourself to express it, the anxiety and anger you're experiencing may decrease. John 14:27 NIV, "Peace I leave with you; my peace I give you. I do not give to you as the world gives. Do not let your hearts be troubled and do not be afraid."

Head Shepherd
P.O.G.
Loving Ministry

Mind

YOUTH

It's time we start to realize the children are the future. At birth, you should start developing them to know who they are in life. Teach them self-love and to respect others. Even in the womb speak words of encouragement over them. When we train a child in the ways of righteousness, they will be someone of importance in society. You have to be that role model for your child, teaching them the ways of Christ. You have to tell them to fight through the worst days of their life to get to the best days of their life. Life might be hard at times, but pursuing what is meaningful to you makes it all worth it. So many of us don't receive the best because we're stuck in our negative pasts. We must let go of all negativity. When you teach them in God's ways, know things will be difficult in life for them. Tell them to let go of their ego and let their heart guide them. Be a good cheer no matter what the enemy throws at us. Keep them connected to God by reading his words to them. Your belief can either raise or lower your vibration. The higher your vibe the better your life. When you surround them with those who love their ambitions, they will be more ambitious and achieve more. Tell them when you focus on possibilities, you will have more opportunities. Keep God first and you may always move forward.

Head Shepherd
P.O.G.
Loving Ministry

www.ingramcontent.com/pod-product-compliance
Lightning Source LLC
LaVergne TN
LVHW091535070526
838199LV00001B/80